I0411143

TIMELESS
WRITINGS
#28
A COMPILATION
FOR MANY WRITERS

TATAY JOBO ELIZES
COMPILER, NOV. 2016

Published: Nov. 2016

Self-Publisher/Compiler/Printer

Tatay Jobo Elizes, born 1934 in Manila, now senior ctizen in Brooklyn, NY. Besides self-publishing, he is busy in piglets dispersal programs for livelihood projects in the Philippines.
.

Acknowledgement

Gratitude and acknowledgment belongs to all contributing writers who gave their permission to compile all articles in a book like this to record history based on timely events that directly or indirectly affect our lives. Copyrights of each article belong to the particular author and he/she is free to re-publish anywhere, without any restriction.

Dedication

I dedicate this book to **all Filipinos** all over the world and to my immediate family, friends and relatives.

This book has the following ISBN numbers:
ISBN-13: 978 - 1539590224
& ISBN-10: 1539590224

Disclaimer:

Free pdf file

FREE reading as ebook is available to interested parties. Just email me at **job_elizes@yahoo.com.**

Booklist Websites
http.//tinyurl.com/mj76ccq
www.jobelizes6.wix.com/mysit

Contents

1.

De Lima's Privilege Speech
(on her ouster from Chairman of Justice Committee)

Senator Leila De Lima

**Published, September 20, 2016,
Rappler.com, WFA, & some Media**

"We must remember that all power, no matter how seemingly absolute, is fleeting. What is permanent is truth and justice"

First of all, congratulations are in order.
Congratulations to Senator Alan Peter Cayetano for his triumphant victory yesterday, and for making me realize that a committee chairmanship is not the end of everything for me as a Senator. No committee chairmanship is worth it, if it means sacrificing my principles and surrendering the causes that I pledged my life to fight for. Many friends and colleagues have told me, if only I did not call out the President on the murderous consequences of his War on Drugs, and decided to be as meek as a sheep, I would not

be in this trouble, and I would still have the Committee chairmanship. As the Bible says, what does it profit a man to gain the whole world, and yet lose his soul?

I choose to keep my soul.

Mr. President, it would take more than a Committee chairmanship, a House inquiry intended to pillory and crucify me, an Ethics Committee complaint based on hearsay, a baseless election protest, everyday tirades from the Secretary of Justice and the Solicitor General, and vicious personal attacks from the President, to take me down. I guess it would take two magazines of an Uzi machine pistol to take me down. As the saying goes, everything has been thrown at me except the kitchen sink. I am still waiting for the kitchen sink.

Mr. President, I did not expect you or the Senators to defend me from the vicious attacks of Malacañang as a person and as an incumbent Senator of the Republic. The least I expected of course is you allow me to defend myself, by myself, without any support whatsoever from the Senate. But for this body to strip me of my Committee in an unprecedented fashion at this point when we have categorical testimony establishing an uncanny similarity between the current phenomenon of the nationwide EJKs and the Davao City EJKs as perpetrated by the Davao Death Squad, was unimaginable. I now resolve to imagine more of what the Presidents allies are capable of.

Sinabi naman po ng Pangulo, hindi siya titigil hanggat ako ay kanyang madurog at mapadapa. With the House inquiry now ongoing, I already warned him, Huwag na po ninyong ituloy Mahal na Pangulo, dahil mapapahiya lamang kayo.

DOJ Secretary Aguirre has also recently pronounced that he is ready to file the criminal complaints against me this week. But these are all based on false and fabricated evidence.

Sino naman po ang mga testigo nila? Mga preso sa Bilibid, mga convicted criminals, DOJ or NBI officials and others who have an axe to grind against me, or those who have skeletons in their closet and are now being pressured to do Malacanangs bidding at the risk of being charged themselves.

Sa puntong ito, gusto kong iparating ang aking pagpapatawad sa lahat ng tumatayo at tatayong witness laban sa akin sa House hearing. Alam ko na kayo ay napilitan at napuwersa lamang para idawit ako sa kung anumang anomalya sa Bilibid, gamit ang panggigipit, blackmail, o marahil pati torture. Ang hindi ko mapapatawad ay ang mga nasa likod nitong pag-imbento ng ebidensiya laban sa akin. May araw din po kayo.

What is the situation now in the Bilibid? I have received reports of inmates and gang leaders being taken by the Special Action Force deployed at the Bilibid for overnight interrogation sessions, which can also be a euphemism for psychological torture, all in an effort to fabricate testimony that I received bribes from drug lords. The National Bilibid Prison under this Administration is now a tropical Gulag. Prisoners are being selected and isolated just to be intimidated into implicating me and to fit the Presidents narrative that I am a drug lord coddler, aside from being the most evil woman in the planet.

Pero ano naman po talaga ang ginawa ko? Wala naman po talaga akong ginawa kung hindi gawin ang trabaho ko. Kahit ang Pangulo minsan naniyang sinambit na kahit siya ang nasa kalagayan ko, ganoon din ang gagawin niya, dahil ginagawa ko lang ang trabaho ko.

Mr. President, I am not the problem. I am not the one giving a bad image to this country before the international media, contrary to the accusation and belief of Senator Cayetano. The problem of this country and this Administration is the extra-judicial killing of more than 3,000 of our countrymen in the past three months, or more than a thousand per month.

Sinabayan pa ito ng bunganga ng Pangulo na walang patumangging magmura ng mga opisyales ng UN at ng mundo, katulad ng Santo Papa, ni Pangulong Obama at ni Sec. Gen. Ban Ki Moon, sa kabila ng pagnanais lang nila na kausapin siya sa kanilang mga agam-agam tungkol sa polisiyang giyera sa droga ng Pangulo. And may I add, the President has already proven that he is more than capable of single-handedly giving a bad image of this country to the whole world in the short span of three months in office. He does not need any help from anybody on that aspect, least ofall from me.

Kaya huwag po ninyong baligtarin ang mundo, na ako ang nagbibigay ng masamang imahe sa Pilipinas dahil hindi ako ang nagmura kay Obama at BanKi Moon. Minsan ay tanggalin naman ninyo ang mga tapaloda ng kabayo sainyong mga mata at medyo punahin naman ninyo kahit konti ang walang kontrol na bunganga ng inyong Pangulong pinagtatanggol.

Mr. President, ito pong mga patayan na ito ang nagbibigay ng masamang imahe sa Pilipinas ngayon. Ganoon na ba tayo kakitid mag-isip para maniwala na hindi papansinin ng mundo o ng international media ang nangyayari sa ating bansa kung wala ang isang Leila De Lima? Ang pagpatay ng mahigit 30 katao araw-araw ay pagpatay pa rin sa mata ng mundo, nandiyan man si Leila De Lima o wala. Sa tingin ba ni Senator Cayetano nasa kanyang tagumpay na matanggal sa akin ang Committee on Justice ay gaganda na antimano ang imahe ng Pilipinas sa mundo? Maari, hindi naman bawal na managinip si Senator Cayetano.

Hindi po ako ang pumapatay sa mga kababayan natin para maibalita sa international media. Hindi po ako ang nag-ra-riding-in-tandem at tumitira sa mga maralitang drug suspects. Hanggang ngayon po ay nandiyan pa rin ang mga salarin na umiikot sa kadiliman ng gabi para itumba ang mga pinagbibintangan na mga kriminal, totoo man silang kriminal o hindi. Maaring iilan sa kanila ay ang mga dating kasamahan ng ating witness nasi Edgar Matobato sa Davao Death Squad. Gusto lang nating malaman kung may katotohanan sa haka-haka na ito, upang sila ay tuluyan ng madakip at mahinto na ang patayan.

There are criticisms from Senator Lacson and Senator Cayetano that I should have vetted the witness first before presenting him in the hearing.

Mr. President, the vetting process of witnesses on the DDS has started since 2009, when as CHR Chairperson I conducted the inquiry on the Davao Death Squad. At that time, we were able to interview and get statements from several DDS members who chose to talk but not to testify for fear of their lives. In fact, as early as 2009,

Edgar Matobato has already been identified by one DDS witness as a companion of said witness in one of his DDS operations.

Nagtutugma po ang ilang mga kuwento sa kuwento ng ating witness na si Edgar Matobato. Katunayan, noong 2009, may mga pangalan nang mga opisyales ng Davao City Police ang lumabas na mga miyembro ng DDS sa heinous crime section ng DCPO, mga pangalan na binanggit na rin ni Matobato sa kanyang testimonya. Ang ilan po sa mga pangalan na ito ay ang mga sumusunod:

SPO4 Arthur Lascanas, P/CInsp Jacy Jay Francia, P/C Insp Fulgencio Pavo, P/C Insp Ronald Lao, SPO3 Jim Tan, SPO4 Sanson Sonny Buenaventura, SPO1 Reynante B. Medina, SPO1 Bienvenido Furog, SPO1 Vivencio Jun Jumawan, SPO2 Enrique Jun Delos Reyes Ayao, SPO3 Jun Laresma, SPO2 Rizalino Bobong G. Aquino, SPO3 Donito Pogi Ubales, SPO1 JunBisnar, SPO1 Gaston Aquino, P/S Supt Isidero Dick Florivel/ Florobel, P/S Supt.Rey Capote, P/S Supt Tony Rivera, P/S Supt Dionisio Abude, Bienvenido Laud, Alvin Laud, Roly Engalia, Arnold Ochavez.

Mr. President, those names compose the core group of the Davao DeathSquad.

Malakas pong ebidensiya ang testimonya ni Edgar Matobato. Hindi ito katulad ng drug matrix na nilabas ng Pangulo na walang gustong umamin sa NBI, PNP, o PDEA kung kanino galing sa kanila ang impormasyon na laman nito. Kung ang pamantayan ng ebidensiya ni Senator Cayetano ay katulad ng drug matrix ng Pangulo na parang dinrawing ng isang dose anyos na bata, di hamak na lampas lampas naman ang testimonya ni Matobato sa pang-dose anyos na standard ng kanyang mahal na Pangulo. Kung minsan po talaga, ang pinakamahirap gisingin ay ang mga nagpapanggap na tulog.

Mr. President, may mga binanggit na pong mga opisyal ng kapulisan ang ating witness. Nasaan na po ang mga opisyal na ito ngayon? Masarap paba ang kanilang tulog sa kabila ng mga binitawang testimonya ni Edgar Matobato? Kung nakakatulog pa sila, marahil sila ay inosente. Pero papaano kung sila ay hindi inosente?

The implication is that we have a group of serial killers and mass murderers right within the ranks of the organization which is supposed to protect and serve the people. I might be jumping to conclusions, but what if it is true? Was the action of the Senate yesterday stripping me of my Committee going to help to uncover the truth, or was it part of the plan to hide the truth? I hope it is not the latter.

I still bear a great amount of respect for my colleagues. I believe that their action yesterday was borne out of an honest desire to diffuse the unnecessary political complexion of the investigation by choosing a more, shall we say, neutral and non-controversial Senator to lead the investigation.

At this point I would like to congratulate Senator Richard Gordon for having been vested with the vote of confidence of the Senate and for accepting the burden of investigating the current phenomenon of extra-judicial killings. I believe in his capability to carry out a serious probe into these incidents and get to the bottom of the killings. I watched his career as a Senator for several terms and I am convinced that he possesses the integrity and the courage not to be cowed by the Executive and act as a mere lackey of Malacañang.

I believe that he is also capable of exercising that impartiality that Senator Cayetano has repeatedly drilled into our heads I am not capable of. I believe that Senator Gordon bears more fortitude and strength than I did, to be able to call out and censure any colleague who transgresses the boundaries of unparliamentary speech when he accuses Liberal Party senators of conspiring to overthrow the President without presenting a single piece of evidence, while accusing me of having pre-judged the EJK investigation on the basis of an eyewitness account coming from a man who claims to have been an original member of the Davao Death Squad, until he was betrayed and framed up by his own comrades for a crime he did not commit.

I am fervently convinced that with his experience and no-nonsense personality, Senator Gordon will be more able to throw out any attempt to badger, harangue, abuse, or otherwise malign a witness by misleading and forcing him to admit that the reason he is testifying is because he was recruited by the Senators of the Liberal Party to trigger the ouster of the President and to put in Malacanang Vice President Leni Robredo whom the witness admitted he barely knows.

This is the kind of pretentious and hypocrite objectivity coming from Senator Cayetano that Senator Gordon will be facing. I wish you good luck, sir. I can tell you it was not a pleasant experience for me. Not at all. You can have the Justice Committee as well as the offensive and unparliamentary antics of Senator Cayetano.

Package deal po yan. On the other hand, you will still have me as a member of the Justice Committee. I promise to behave and not give you a hard time. A Senator Cayetano is enough. I will not bother you with another obnoxious personality in your hearings in the Justice Committee.

May nakausap po akong taxi driver noong isang araw. Ang sabi niya ay parang magulo na naman sa bansa natin, katulad ng pagkagulo ng bansa sa ilalim ng ilang mga nakaraang administrasyon. Patayan dito, bombahan doon, mga bangkay na naglipana sa daan, mga barilan ng mga riding-in-tandem, mga abuso ng mga kapulisan sa mga pag-raid at pag-Tokhang sa mga urban poor areas, etcetera, etcetera.

Sa totoo lang po, wala akong nakausap na taxi driver. Ginaya ko lang po ang istilo ng pagkwento ni Senator Cayetano para patunayan niya na ang Pilipinas ay kasing-safe na ng bansang Singapore. Sa totoo lang po, medyona bilaukan ako sa sinabi na iyon ni Senator Cayetano kahit nandoon na ako sa katahimikan ng aking opisina. Kasing-tahimik at kasing-ligtas na raw tayo katulad ng Singapore.

Hindi pa po ako nakapunta sa Singapore. Pero kung kasing-tahimik ng Singapore ang Pilipinas, kailangan din bang may bumubulagta na mahigit 30 tao kada araw sa Singapore para sila ay maging ligtas? Kailangan din ba nilang mag-Tokhang para malipol ang mga mapanganib na mga pusher at addict at malinis ang mga komunidad ng masasamang elemento? Kailangan ba nilang padanakin ang dugo sa kanilang mga kalsada upang mapanatag ang mga tao na may ginagawa ang gobyerno para mapuksa ang kriminalidad? Kailangan din bang may mamatay na apat o limang-taong gulang na Singaporean sa kamay ng mga vigilante dahil ang lolo o tatay nila ay mga markadong pusher o adik?

O ibang pamamaraan ba ang ginawa ng Singapore para mapanalig ang tao sa respeto sa kaayusan at sa pag-hahari ng batas? Ang pamamaraan ng patayan para magkaroon ng katahimikan ay magdudulot lang ng katahimikan ng sementeryo. Papunta na po tayo doon, dahil unti-unti ng pinupuno ng Administrasyong ito ang ating mga sementeryo sa kanyang pagkibit-balikat kung hindi man tahasang pang-enganyo sa isang marahas na landas tungo sapag puksa ng literal sa mga kriminal.

The point is, Senator Cayetano wants to impress upon us the Singapore-like safety of our communities in the middle of all these killings with anecdotes. His proof that we are safe consists of anecdotal taxi driver stories. In the meantime, his President has just declared a State of National Emergency due to the existence of Lawless Violence. For the first time since the eve of the declaration of Martial Law 44 years ago to the day today, the country has not come close to such an admission by the State that it is incapable of enforcing order in society, that the President has to resort to his extraordinary commander-in-chief powers under the Constitution in order to maintain public safety, peace and order.

So are we in a State of Safety, as claimed by Senator Cayetano? Or are we in a State of Lawlessness, as declared by the President?

Safe lawlessness, or lawless safety? Ang tawag po doon sa salitang Inggles ay oxymoron, with emphasis on moron.

Senator Cayetanos anecdotes will not pass any known academic standard to prove his proposed thesis that our countrymen feel safe. I for one do not feel safe, what with the President unleashing the might and power of the whole Executive Branch, the other half of Congress, and 1/24 of the Senate to go after me and destroy me, a single Senator from Bicol who wants nothing else in the world but to be and play with her dogs at home and to see that the killings stop and justice be done to those who already fell during the night.

The next time Senator Cayetano recites his now famous anecdotes about how safe we are, maybe he can include my own story. Definitely it is not a story of being safe. It is the story of being the first target of a new McCarthyism in our time, of being singled out by the powers-that-be for daring to think differently and to advocate passionately for what onebelieves in.

Matagal na po itong linya ng kanyang mga bayarang trolls sa social media. Kapag hindi ka Pro-Duterte, ikaw ay drug lord coddler, ikaw ay pusher, ikaw ay isang adik. Ito po ang bagong komunistang panakot sa ating panahon ngayon: Ang Adik. Kapag hindi ka sumamba kay Poong Duterte, ikaw ay adik, dahil adik lang ang hindi sumasamba kay Poong Duterte.

Bakit po tayo nahantong sa ganito? Na ang mga nagnanais ng maayos at naayon sa batas na laban sa kriminalidad ay mga nababansagan na mga adik, at nawawalan ng kalayaan na sumalungat sa pamamaraan ng tinatawag napagbabago sa pamamagitan ng kaliwat kanang patayan? At ngayon na napapalapit tayo sa paghubad ng katotohanan na ang ganitong pangyayari ay naganap na sa Davao City, ay biglang idedeclare na vacant ang Komiteng dumidinig sa paksa ng patayan dahil lang sa sinabi ng pinakadakilang tagapagtanggol ng Pangulo sa Senado, at sinegunduhan ng isang Senador nagaling sa mga mahihirap, mga mahihirap na ngayon ay walang tigil na Tinotokhang ng mga pulis.

On a personal note, I do not know where all of this will end for me, in the midst of the House inquiry, the Ethics Committee complaint, the election protest, the DOJ persecution, and the Presidents attacks. Honestly, this is all the fault of President Gloria Macapagal-Arroyo, when she appointed me as Chair of the Commission on Human Rights, where I learned the value of human life and human dignity, regardless of ones station in life. This is also the fault of President Benigno S. Aquino III, when he appointed me as Secretary of Justice, where I learned to fight the abuse of power, corruption, and have taken to heart the principle that peace is the work of justice.

Ang kapayapaan ay bunga ng hustisya. Walang kapayapaan kung walang hustisya.

Pasensiya na po ang ating mga kababayan kung natuto ako sa CHR at sa DOJ na pahalagaan ang buhay ng bawat tao, ang karapatan na magkaroon ng paglilitis bago patawan ng karampatang kaparusahan, at ang seguridad ng lahat na maging tahimik sa loob ng kanilang tahanan.

Gaano man kaliit ang dampa, ang bawat tahanan ay palasyo ng namamahay doon. Iyan ang itinuro sa atin sa batas. Kung gaano kabuo ang respeto ng mga pulis na nagTotokhang sa Forbes Park at sa Dasmarinas Village, ganoondin dapat ang respeto na pinapakita nila sa mga Tinotokhang nila sa mga maralitang nakatira sa mga tabing-ilog at estero. Mayaman man o mahirap, kapag Tinokhang mo, dapat ay pantay-pantay. Huwag yung mga berdugong pulis ang ipapadala sa mga dampa sa estero, at mga pulis na sumasali sa modelling contest ang ipapadala sa Forbes Park.

Sasabihin na naman ni Senator Cayetano na hindi naman mga nagmomodel na pulis ang pinapadala sa Forbes Park. Figure of Speech lamang po iyon, hindi dapat intindihin ng literal.

I became CHR Chair and DOJ Secretary not because I sought those positions to which I was appointed. One can say that these were all accidents of history. It is only this position that I hold now that I chose to work hard for to get by tirelessly campaigning and eventually being elected by more than 14 million Filipino voters.

Kaya mahalaga po sa akin ang posisyon na ito, dahil katulad ninyo mgakapwa ko senador, pinagsikapan at pinaghirapan ko itong ipagkatiwala sa akin ng mga botanteng Pilipino. Ginagampanan ko lamang ang aking tungkulin bilang isang kandidato na humarap sa mga tao ng may platapormang karapatang pantao at hustisya, dahil minarapat nila na iboto ako sa pag-asang ang programang iyon ang aking dadalhin dito sa Senado.

Ito po ang programang dala ko ngayon, mga mahal kong kababayan na bumotosa akin. Ninais *ninyo na ito ang programang dalhin ko. Kung sa pagnanais kong isulong ang programang ito ay tatanggalin ako sa pagka-pinuno ng Komite ng Hustisya at Karapatang Pantao, ay parang hinubad na rin nila sa akin ang mahalagang bahagi ng mandatong iyon.*

Pero tatalima ako sa desisyon ng Senado. Hindi naman dito natatapos ang laban. Nag-iba lang ang anyo at posisyon ng mga magkakatunggali, pero malinaw pa rin ang adhikain at pananalig na sa bandang huli, ang hustisya at karapatan ng bawat mamamayan ang mananaig, hindi ang dikta ngkapangyarihan.

Sa Roma, noong unang panahon, pinagdiriwang ang mga heneral na matagumpay na sumakop ng mga ibang bayan sa pamamagitan ng isang parada, kung saan nakasakay ang Heneral sa isang karyote na hila ng apat na puting kabayo habang papasok sa siyudad ng Roma. Sa likod niya ay isang alipin, na mayhawak na ginintuang koronang laurel sa itaas ng ulo ng Heneral. Sa kahabaan ng prusisyon, walang ibang ginawa ang alipin kung hindi bumulong sa tenga ng Heneral ng mga katagang Respice post te! Hominem tememento!

Tumingin ka sa likod mo, at huwag kalimutan na ikaw ay isa lamangtao.

Hindi Diyos, tao.

Tao ka lamang.

Mr. President, my fellow Senators, on the eve of the 44th Anniversary of the Declaration of Martial Law, we must remember that all power, no matter how seemingly absolute, is fleeting. What is permanent is truth and justice.

Ang lahat ng kapangyarihan, gaano man kalawak ang nasasakupan, ay naglalaho rin sa panahon. Ang tanging nagtatagal sa habang panahon ay katotohanan at katarungan.

Iyan po ang sumpa ng mga may hawak sa kapangyarihan, katulad natin. Maglalaho din yan sa daloy ng panahon. Pero ang katotohanan at katarunganang mananatili. Katulad po ng sinapit ng Rehimeng Marcos noong 1986, ang lahat ng diktadura ay may hangganan din. Marahil hindi ngayon, pero ang panahon ng lahat ng may kapangyarihan ay may hangganan.

Marami po sa atin ang pamilyar sa kwento na ito ng Roma tungkol sa alipin na nasa likod ng matagumpay na Heneral na mananakop. Ang hindi pa alam ngmarami, na ang kinakatakutan ng Heneral ay si FORTUNA, na kung tawagin ay ang berdugo ng lasing na tagumpay: THE BUTCHER OF GLORY.

Iubetque eosdem respicere similis medicina linguae, ut sit exorata atergo Fortuna gloriae carnifex.

Binabadya ng mga kataga ang matagumpay na Heneral: tumingin ka salikod, upang mapaamo mo si Fortuna, ang berdugo ng lasing natagumpay.

Sa mga Heneral ng tagumpay at kapangyarihan sa ating panahon: si Fortuna ay inyong kapalaran, nagbabadya na ang lahat ng hawak ninyo ngayon ay maglalaho sa panahon. Mapaamo nyo man siya, siya at siya pa rin ang kikitil sa inyong pagkalasing sa panandaliang kapangyarihan at tagumpay.

Maraming salamat po.

2.
Silent No More

Sen. Leila De Lima

Dateline, Oct. 14, 2016

(Speech by Leila M. de Lima during "A Forum on Women's Life, Dignity, and Democracy" at Miriam College, Katipunan Avenue, last October 14, 2016)

Thank you so much Miriam College, particularly the organizer, the WAGI, Miriam College Women and Gender Institute; concerned women's CSOs and activists. Thank you, of course, to Ms. Lynda Garcia, for her very kind and gracious words in her introduction; to Ms. Melanie Reyes, very powerful opening remarks; and of course to my dear, favourite, best professor during my La Salle days, Dr. Professor Soc Reyes, the ever sharp and energetic professor, now my number one fan; other professors here in Miriam College; Dr. Marge Acosta, Jerry Jurisprudencia; Atty. Cristine Lao; Prof. Lynda Garcia; Dr. Loreta Castro; Ms. Valerie Buenaventura—*wow, ang* *sarap pa lang maging professor dito.* Or is it because it's an exam week? Is it an exam week? *(Laughter) Yun pala.* Now I know. *Sino pa ba, baka may mga nakakalimutan ako?* Who? Jonas David; where are you? Hi Jonas. I understand. Dr. Parayno. Where's Dr. Parayno? Hi. I understand these are predominantly Psychology students and International Studies students, also Mass Communications. I was sitting with a pretty lady here, and she told me she is a Masscom student, and I told her I'm sure you'll become a woman anchor in any of our networks. Thank you so much, *maraming, maraming salamat po sa inyong lahat sa napakamainit na pagbati, pag-welcome sa akin.* This is such a respite, a welcome break for me.

You know when I wake up in the morning, I would not know what kind of day I'll be facing. You know I live by the day. *Hindi ko talaga alam kung ano na naman ang mga maririnig ko, makikita ko sa diyaryo, makikita sa social media,* although, I avoid going over my Facebook nowadays. Let me start by making this clear—lest some of you, or many of you have started to believe, or are in fact, believing everything that they see on television, on the social media—those hearings in the House of Representatives, I am not the bad and evil woman, or slut that they are trying to portary in the past few weeks. I have not partied or slept with any drug convict. I have not received anything from a drug convict or a drug lord, or anyone else. I have not received P2 million in one meeting with one of those convicts at the office of a former director. I have not received P3 million a week, a month—I think that's what they said—since 2012. I did not receive P10 million from anyone, let alone from a drug convict. I did not receive P5 million in two or three occasions in my house from a former official of BuCor. I have not benefited from the drug trade. I am not the Queen of the Drug Trade of the Bilibid. I am not the mother of these drug lords. And I am not one who won as a member of the Senate and has turned this country into a narco-state, because in the first place, our country is far from being a narco-state.

And yes, as a human being, as a woman, I have frailties, I have weaknesses, I have certain flaws as a woman, I've made mistakes in my personal life, and I've always considered my personal life as a private matter. It's a sacred thing to me. But now, they've been intruding and encroaching into my privacy. Yes, I made mistakes, and when I do make mistakes in my personal life, I pick up the pieces and move on. But never did I betray my country. I want that made clear because that's what I fear that some of you may have started to believe the relentless, vicious attacks being launched and led by the most powerful man in this country.

With that note, allow me please to now give you my core messages for today's forum. And I thank the organizers of this forum, the women's groups, particularly the group of Prof. Soc because we've been doing this precisely to generate much awareness among the populace, especially you, young people, young students, beautiful students of Miriam. We need to raise awareness on our fight for the truth, fight for justice, fight for human rights, women's rights, and democracy. Human rights because of the spate of extrajudicial killings we are seeing on a daily basis. Women's rights because of the slut-shaming that I'm being subjected to for being a poster girl, allegedly a poster girl. And democracy because of the muzzling of dissent.

I'm Exhibit A simply because I'm a vocal critic of the anti-human rights policies of this presidency, of this administration, particularly extrajudicial killings. I'm being subjected to these unprecedented attacks on my person, on my character, and on my credibility. Their whole agenda is to crush and break my spirit so that no one would listen to me anymore. Our democracy is in peril. And that's why I'm doing this. *Halos walang nakikinig sa akin sa Senado* so I might as well get out of the Senate halls and reach out to you, in the hope that you would listen and open your minds.

So a good Friday morning to everyone. Good morning. It's quite an honor and pleasure to be here as a guest speaker in today's *Buhay at Dignidad* Forum, more so these days because this has been very trying times for me, a very difficult, very challenging times. It is a period in my life when finding a role to fill—other than that of a woman who has fallen victim to a constant barrage of attacks from no less than the most powerful man in the land and those who share his vengeful passion—has become of utmost importance in order to hold on to some vestige of personal dignity, and hope for the future of our country. Even my time in the office is not much of a respite from the stress of unmitigated attacks, which is why times like this—when I get to go out and meet with people, especially the young, face-to-face, see the faces of the people I am fighting for—are even more precious to me than they have ever been before.

So thank you. Thank you for the organizers, thank you for media by the way, for those who are around. They've been following me and I don't mind. *(Laughter)* And in doing so, giving this woman enough strength to fight another day. Indeed, at a time when sexism has once again reared its ugly and despicable head in the form of a President who thinks nothing of telling a woman to kill herself—all for the sin of daring to stand up against men on the issue of the spate of extrajudicial killings—the fight to protect the sanctity of human life, and to retain some level of dignity in the face of oppression and inhumanity, has been a daily struggle.

But, let me tell you: it does not surprise me—not even a little bit—that the most immediate and most vocal support I have received are from women. My detractors may hide behind the power of their office, or in the anonymity of the internet or of unrecorded cellphone numbers in order to hurl insults, misinformation, outright lies and even death threats against me. There are also many who have sent their support, but more discreetly in order not to draw attention to themselves. These are well meaning, and much appreciated supporters, but they are nothing like the people—most of them women, and some notable men—who have spoken out publicly in my defense or, more to the point, against behavior that alternates between vile maliciousness, playground bullying, and professional trolling. I will admit that there was a moment in the last three months when I began to doubt whether I will ever be vindicated, whether in this lifetime or beyond. Yes, I must admit that this human rights advocate and former Secretary of

Justice was made to doubt if justice will ever be served. Look at all those complaints, why file those complaints to the DOJ when the master of the fakery is now the head of that institution. They must file it directly with the Office of the Ombudsman. But I have people like the women and the few men present here for restoring my faith in mankind.

And speaking of mankind, let's take a bit of a break from the daytime soap opera-esque turn that might life has taken, and venture a bit into non-Rodrigo Duterte and EJKs territory. No, I can't even talk about one of the most internationally-relevant event that is about to happen outside the Philippines in the next few weeks because, then, I would be venturing into Trump territory. God forbid there's another mysoginistic leader emerging in the world because this would just be trading one chauvinistic mammal for another. No, let's step even farther. Back in 1950s, Italian physicist Enrico Fermi—I don't know if there are students of Physics here—posed a question that has become known as the so-called "Fermi Paradox". *Simple lang ang tanong niya: sa dinamirami ng mga bituin sa buong kalawakan na katulad ng ating araw, kung saan marami sa kanila ay mas matanda pa kaysa sa ating araw; at sa taas ng probabilidad na ilan sa mga bituing iyon ay may kahit isang kasamang planeta na katulad ng ating mundo, na marahil ay may sibilisasyon na natuto nang makapaglalakbay sa kalawakan—bakit hindi pa nila tayo nabibisita?* That's the Fermi Paradox. Basically, Fermi was wondering, with such a high probability of alien life capable of interstellar travel: where is everybody?

A few days ago, it was reported that another physicist, Brian Cox, has proposed an answer to the "paradox", but his answer is more from the field of political science than physics, and it paints a grim picture for humanity. He said that "One solution to the Fermi paradox is that it is not possible to run a world that has the power to destroy itself and that needs global collaborative solutions to prevent that."[1] In other words, he's saying that civilizations politically implode and exterminate themselves before they can achieve interstellar travel because their members are far too often more prepared to kill each other rather than help and cooperate with each other. Part of his hypothesis is to suggest that maybe the fields of science and engineering inevitably develop faster than our political expertise, which will lead us to disaster. Basically, saying that we gain the ability to make weapons of mass destruction—and eventually, weapons of mass extinction—faster than our ability to gain the enlightenment and wisdom not to use it on each other. He then warned that—I'm talking about Brian Cox—"It may be that the growth of science and engineering inevitably outstrips the development of political expertise, leading to disaster. We could be approaching that position."

Yes, it's just a hypothesis, but, you must admit, it's an interesting food for thought, at the very least, and perhaps a cause for alarm if we bother to read the signs of the times. It can't be a coincidence that Cox made public his hypothesis in the year 2016, the year when the next space race was declared by the CEO of Boeing, the airlines, the company which "once helped the US beat the

Soviet Union in the race to the moon,"[2] by challenging the billionaire-engineer/investor Elon Musk, the man behind SpaceX, Tesla Motors, and SolarCity, to a race to bring human beings to Mars; which is also the year when the world seems to have been turned upside politically—with misogynistic, and narcissistic authoritarians, so-called populist leaders finding their way back to power, ironically, on the back of the masses through so-called democratic processes, by capitalizing on the terror being wreaked by extremist groups. Let's all think about that. The signs are telling us to brace for a rough ride.

For 2016 is definitely the year we start truly feeling insecure in the possibility of nuclear codes falling into, if not already in the hands of dictatorial sociopaths with itchy fingers, short tempers, and no impulse control. And why do I bring these up here, in this forum on Women's Life, Dignity and Democracy? Because 2016 is also the year when there has been an unacceptable resurgence in sexist behavior that is not just a sign of political immaturity, but is actually intentionally meant to undermine the role and influence of women in society—which could very well be what will ultimately give free reign to the destructive forces in our midst to completely destroy our political structure and our very humanity. *Kapag mga babae na kasi, iba. 'Di ba, at least ang mga babae ang puwedeng mag-isip at gumawa ng paraan para hindi mangyayari ang mga ganyang kadiliman.* Just last year, an audience in this very academic institution hosted a forum—I don't know if you were there.

I think some or many of you were here—where the key guest was Chilean President Michelle Bachelet, who "acknowledged the Philippine progress and efforts to recognize women's roles in the creation of a just, peaceful, and prosperous society despite them being silenced and overshadowed by men." She even went on to say that "[t]here is no doubt about the role played by the women of the Katipunan in 1896, and the contribution of the Katipuneras of Miriam College in the fight against the Marcos dictatorship." And she lauded our nation's progress as "the only Asian country that has been able to completely close the gender gap in education and health, and is the only one placed in the top 10 of the [Global Gender Gap Report 2014]."[3] Because we are supposed to be number 7 as the most gender-equal nation in the world, and number one in Asia, and even in Asia-Pacific.

Ironic. I, myself, a year ago would have said that, in spite of the gaps that still need to be closed, especially in terms of those created by poverty, Filipino women are in a globally enviable position because of all the factors that could hinder our personal growth and inhibit our potential for achieving our goals, gender is probably near the bottom of the list. I would have said that women are seen as every bit as important as men in this country. I would have said that. I could have said the same thing just three months ago—after all, I was elected into office, just like many of my fellow female elected officials. And, to a large extent, I would still say that this holds true even today. The only difference is that the few who still maintain backwards thinking—including a President who unapologetically catcalls female members of the press and then blames them for not accepting the "gesture" as a compliment, the same President who makes jokes about it being a pity that a beautiful missionary woman was raped and killed without the Mayor having a go at her first, and other "boys' locker room" jokes about no one listening to a female President[4]—are so powerful and so prominently featured in the media that these little toxic drops of poison are threatening to compromise the integrity of the whole well.

That is the challenge we face today. It's not that we're facing full-blown social marginalization—it is that this fast-growing and spreading brand of old school misogyny is the type of creeping marginalization and sexism that could very well overwhelm us before we know it. There was a recently published article that questions the validity of my alleged status as a so-called "poster child" of victims of misogyny, saying that I am going through my travails in the last few months, not because I am a woman, but because I am getting payback—according to that journalist—for the offenses I have allegedly committed against others. First of all, does that make my situation any better? That I am being publicly shamed and politically persecuted because for the last eight years I tried to do my job the best I could? If I truly stepped on the toes of some people, and they are seeking their vindication, is slut-shaming me really the way to exact justice in this country? I would hope not. Secondly, yes, it is true. I have been very lucky in my life up to this point.

True, I have held very powerful posts. I must point out, however, that my post as a Senator today, though it is still a position of influence, it not truly a position of great power though, as many of you may have seen, judging by how my efforts have been so readily shot down by some of my colleagues in the Senate. But, more importantly, to become a victim of misogyny, the reason for the attacks need not be because of gender, if the manner in which one is attacked is tantamount to getting stabbed over and over with the dagger of sexism. The fallacy in the reasoning is no different from what is truly getting in the way of understanding the problem of EJKs. In determining whether or not a particular case is an EJK, it does not matter whatsoever that the person killed was truly a drug suspect, or a drug user, or a drug lord. The identity of the victim or the motive for the killing are not elements of the crime of murder. They are irrelevant to the question of whether he or she was the victim of EJK. What matters is whether the person was killed—for lack of a better word—"lawfully" in the absence of death penalty, an acceptable reason for killing a drug suspect is self-defense.

And, under our laws, self-defense, please no make mistake about that, self-defense is a very exacting grounds to prove: there must be aggression on the part of the victim, reasonable necessity of the means employed to prevent or repel it, and lack of sufficient provocation on the part of the person defending himself. Those are the only questions that need to be asked. In the case of misogyny, while being discriminated against or treated unfairly or disrespectfully simply by reason of one's gender is itself misogyny, unfortunately, that is not the only way by which misogyny can rear its ugly head. The manner and not just the motive *or* reason could also make malicious and unfair treatment a case of misogyny.

In my case, obviously I owe my predicament, not to my gender, but my sheer audacity to do my job, first as Chairperson of the Commission on Human Rights and thereafter, as Secretary of Justice. True, it is perfectly understandable that there are people who will hold a grudge against me—especially powerful people who were the subject of investigations into various high profile cases, who are now, apparently, out to "get me". But it is not the motive for trying to destroy me that makes the issue of sexism and misogyny relevant. It is the manner by which they set out to destroy me—with no less than their revered leader calling me an immoral woman, a woman of the world, who should be ashamed of myself and therefore, should go hang myself, while he, himself is a self-confessed unfaithful womanizer. Proud womanizer. If that is not sexism, what is? If so-called journalists cannot follow the logic, how can we expect the general public?

How can we make our children understand what is wrong with that scenario? How can we hope that our young students, our daughters will not fall victim to the same situations will know how to recognize those situations and, should they be unfortunate enough to encounter it, be able to adequately defend themselves from it? How do we teach our sons to be better than their President or their congressmen? We can do that by not being cowed into silence. *Sabi nga ho ni Fr. Robert Reyes doon sa kanyang homily noong isang linggo, doon sa Misa Para sa Katotohanan at*

Katurangan, it's not only the evil of the killings and the abuse of power that we're seing now, but there's also the evil of silence. We cannot be cowed into silence. By making sure that our voices and views are heard that this so-called democracy, at least, still has some hope for succeeding, and not disintegrating into the rule of an angry, unthinking mob. They will call us shrill. They will label us as naggers. As irrational women who have to be told to "calm down" even while they themselves are melting down after their masculinity is questioned. But that is part of the battle we have to fight.

Remember, the fight is not just for women. It is for our collective humanity. That maybe, maybe, we really could achieve political maturity that will help prevent us from killing each other, more than we already currently are. I know it's a cliché, but I also know that there is truth to the role of women as nurturers. We need to nurture our own dignity, in order to win back our true democracy. What we have now is mob rule and madness, if we go by the sheer inability of people to see what the problem is. It is not true democracy, for genuine democracy presupposes that we actually have the mental capacity and the will to make informed decisions by actually first understanding the issues. That is another thing that physicist Cox missed. Our problem is not so much that our capacity for scientific learning outstrips our capacity for political learning. It is only that we keep forgetting what we learn, *ang bilis kasi nating makalimot,* and the new generation has to learn them again and again— often the hard way. There is a difference between how we pass on scientific knowledge, or how such knowledge retain their integrity; and how we pass on political wisdom, which is always the subject of doubt and skepticism.

I don't know if we do have political wisdom. Perhaps it is time that we find innovative ways to teach our young people, our children the lessons of the past, so that they don't have to re-learn them by making the same mistakes that we did. Look at all the historical revisionism that is being foisted on us on the issue of the Marcos burial at the *Libingan ng mga Bayani.* That's the life of a woman: while men seem to think of only the here and now, with little regard for the chain of intended and unintended consequences, we, as nurturers, always have to think ahead and think deeply. That's why we have intuition, woman's intuition. *Tayo lang po meron niyan. Wala sila niyan.* Let's use it intelligently. That is why we cannot afford to be silenced. Let's put a stop to the evil of silence. We must speak, and we must speak, not just as human beings, but specifically as women. While I never asked to be the poster child for any sort of victimization—*Hindi ko talaga na-imagine sa buong buhay ko na magiging biktima rin pala ako ng human rights violation. Akala ko tagapagtanggol lang ako ng mga nabibiktima ng human rights violations.* Because you know, my role is that of an advocate being so much more safe and comfortable a role than as a victim—I am not one to let a good opportunity to be an agent of positive change go to waste. And therefore, I thank all of you again for this opportunity. It has been a welcome break from the daily grind I have been going through, while at the same time, affording me the chance to turn lemons into lemonade by seeing the upside of my situation. *Hangga't kaya ko, kakayanin ko. Hangga't kaya ko, lalaban po ako. Maraming salamat po.*

ooOOoo

3.

Department of Clarification and Explanation (Excerpts)

Greg B. Macabenta

Greg B. Macabenta is an advertisingand communications man shuttling between San Francisco and Manila and providing unique insights on issues from both perspectives.
gregmacabenta@hotmail.com

Dateline, Oct 9, 2016, Posted online by:
<A1.Moonglow@shaw.ca>

"I object to violence because when it appears to do good, the good is only temporary; the evil it does is permanent." - Mahatma Gandhi

Addi Batica, a Fil-Am relative from Samar and Minnesota, has a brilliant solution to the apparent confusionin the government of President Rodrigo Duterte, which The Philippine Star columnist Dick Pascual referred to in a recent piece, "Change is Coming: Flip-Flop pa more."

With unveiled sarcasm, Pascual wrote: "We've all been told by then presidential candidate

Rodrigo Duterte -- Change is Coming! After that fair warning, why should we now be surprised by President Duterte's changing his mind whenever he gets caught in a corner after blurting out something unintended, preposterous, not presidential, or simply rude?

"His flip-flopping statements are too many to be quoted here. But they are recorded in news stories, in reports of embassies and banks, in Google, and social media, or etched in people's minds. Subjects range from political rhetoric to foreign relations."

Duterte's apologists, explainers, clarifiers and interpreters, euphemistically referred to as spokespersons, have been scrambling all over the place trying to perform their functions. But their boss -- or, more appropriately, their ward -- has been shooting off one controversial statement after another with such frequency that Batica believes the government needs to formally create a new full-time office for it, with Cabinet rank:

The Department of Clarification and Explanation.

I wholeheartedly endorse this idea. The new department can have several bureaus under it. The **Bureau of Interpretation's** principal function will be to interpret to the Filipino people and to the international community the meaning of Duterte's flood of invectives and profanities.

Foreign Affairs Secretary Perfecto Yasay, Jr. could take on this function as a concurrent position, assuming the law allows it. Otherwise, he would do well to give up the foreign affairs portfolio and assume the newpost.

The reason for this is because Yasay claims to be one of the fortunate individuals who were close to Duterte in college and were the objects of Duterte's favorite expression, "P*t***ina mo!"

While the ignorant and naïve international media have taken it to mean, "Your mother is a whore" or conversely, "You are a son of a bitch," Yasay has clarified that this vulgarity is actually a way of expressing fondness and affection.

One can imagine a situation where Duterte would tell Yasay, "P*t***ina mo!" and Yasay would respond with, "Thanks Rody, I like you too! P*t***ina mo rin!" followed by a fraternal embrace.

I would, however, caution people who want to get into Yasay's good graces not to use the same fraternal greeting on him these days. That expression may have already been elevated to presidential rank, meaning, only the President of the country can use it on Yasay.

But to go back to the subject of the new Cabinet office, the Bureau of Clarification and Explanation will have under it the Office of Denials which will be charged with pointing out that when Duterte makes a momentous statement, e.g, that he wants the United States to pull out of Mindanao, the new bureau will deny that Duterte really means the US should leave Mindanao or the entire Philippines but that Duterte is really expressing genuine concern for the safety of American soldiers, which is why he wants them out of the Mindanao danger zone.

The Office of Denial will also deny that Duterte does not like America anymore and will, in fact, clarify that Duterte is committed to honoring existing treaties between the Philippines and the US.

Another bureau will be the Bureau of Buck-Passing and Counterattack. This bureau will take care of blaming the media for misinterpreting Duterte'snoble intentions.

A very important office is the Bureau of Apologies and Interpretation. This key function has, in the meantime, been undertaken by Duterte himself in connection with the furor over his reference to Hitler in announcing his intention to slaughter three million drug lords, pushers, and addicts.

Following is an account by GMA News that illustrates how important this new bureau is, such that the President has to perform the function himself in the meantime:

"President Rodrigo Duterte on Sunday apologized to the Jewish community, following his pronouncements last week saying he was willing to do to the country's criminals what Hitler did to the Jews.

"'I would like to make it clear that there was never an intention on my part to derogate the memory of the six million Jews murdered by the Germans... I apologize profoundly and deeply to the Jewish [community],' Duterte said during the opening ceremony of the Masskara Festival in Bacolod City.

"This comes after Duterte last week said he was willing to slaughter three million addicts in the country under his intensified campaign against illegal drugs.

"'Hitler massacred three million Jews. Now, there are three million drug addicts (in the

Philippines. I'd be happy to slaughter them,' hetold reporters in Davao.

"'At least if Germany had Hitler, the Philippines would have... You know my victims, I would like to be, all criminals, to finish the problemof my country and save the next generation from perdition,' he added."

The GMA report further quoted Duterte: "'It was never my intention but the problem was I was criticized using Hitler,' he said.

"This was the same explanation made by Malacañang on Saturday, saying that the President was merely 'addressing the negative comparison that people made between him and Hitler.'"

"'The President's reference to the slaughter was an oblique deflection of the way he has been pictured as a mass murderer, a Hitler, a label he rejects,' Presidential Spokesperson Ernesto Abella said in a statement."

The Duterte government badly needs to activate this new Department of Clarification and Explanation before things go out of hand. At this point, the European Union, the United Nations, the US and Australia have begun to bristle at Duterte's "colorful" language, to use a diplomatic description by President Barack Obama.

Columnist Dick Pascual listed Duterte's flip-flopping in hiscolumn:

"They include his statements/promises to: end crime and corruptionin six months or he would resign if he failed; expel US servicemen from Mindanao; pullout the Philippines from the United Nations; issue a Freedom of Information executive order on his first day in Malacañang, confront President Obama on the latter's statements about human rights when they meet in Vientiane; put an early stop to 'endo' or the contractualization of workers.

"Is this fickleness of mind -- called by some as FMD or Foot-in-the-Mouth Disease -- a symptom of something seriously wrong? We hope not."

Setting up a new Cabinet department to meet exigencies is nothing new. I wrote about it in a piece back in 2011:

"In a book by Charles Osgood entitled, Funny Letters from Famous People, one of the entries is a memo issued by President Harry S. Truman in 1947. Truman apparently wrote it in jest. But in the Philippines, Jokers are often taken seriously.

"Wrote Truman: 'I have appointed a Secretary of Semantics -- a most important post. He is to furnish me 40 to 50 dollar words. Tell me how to say yes and no in the same sentence without a contradiction. He is to tell me the combination of words that will put me against inflation in San Francisco and for it in New York. He is to show me how to keep silent-- and say everything. You can very well see how he can save me an immense amount of worry.'"

But the Department of Semantics pales in importance compared to the urgent need for a Department of Clarification and Explanation.

I understand that the need for such a cabinet office has been such that a concerned member of Congress plans to file a bill that will attach the office of Communications Secretary Martin Andanar and palace spokesman Abella to the Bureau of Fire Protection.

According to the congressman, "Kailangan ng gobyerno ng taga-patayng sunog."

ooOOoo

4.

Just the Facts vs. Attack the West to Appease the East

Mercy Rivera Abad

member - upscaloop@yahoogroups.com

Dateline, Oct. 1, 2016

Just received this. Sharing to enlighten us with the facts - ATTACK THE WEST TO APPEASE THE EAST

In the latest installment of Duterte's rants, he praises China for their "generosity" to the Philippines – something about promised materials for rehab centers. Then he attacks the US for selling only 2 FA-50 fighters without bullets or missiles. Plus says the US only "gives you principles and nothing else."

Let's check the facts before his statements become gospel truths.

1. The two FA-50 fighters were bought from South Korea not USA. Duterte is misinformed. Or he is deliberately misinforming.

2. In the aftermath of super-typhoon Yolanda, China pledged a total of $2M in aid, dwarfed by furniture-maker Ikea that pledged $2.7M. US initially pledged $20M in aid, but delivered $90.9M. Among the first responders to Tacloban were helicopters of the US military who helped restore operations at the airport to allow aid to flow thru. So much for "principles and nothing else"

3. ODA (official development aid) grants portfolio of the Philippines stood at $3.19B in 2014. Of this total, 36.1% of grants were from USA. 5.2% by Japan. Only 0.18% by China. USA grants were 200x more than China. Many of the USAID projects are in health, education, community development – the precise interventions into the root causes of drug abuse

4. Excluded from these ODA are the military assistance which is increasing. USA and Japan are once again the biggest donors.

5. Based on 2015 data, Japan is our biggest merchandise export market at $12.5B. Followed by US at 8.6B. Chinas at 7.3B. We have a trade surplus with Japan of $6.5B and US at $0.6B. We have a trade deficit with China of $1.9B

6. US is our biggest service export market via BPO industry. BPOs are estimated to generate $25B revenues in 2016 ($55B by 2020). 77% of our BPO market is US-bound. That $30B growth in BPO from 2016 to 2020 is greater than any manufacturing or export-led growth possible.

BPO is the sunrise industry for the Philippines where we have clear competitive advantage (language, adaptability, time zone) versus the rest of the world. US is the main market now & in the future

7. Philippines received $25.8B in remittances in 2015. Biggest contributor was USA at 31.2%. China at around 0.2% only. US remittances are 127x bigger than China.

8. In terms of net foreign direct investments, USA contributed 34% of all FDI in 2011-15. Japan came next at 23.7%. China was far behind at only 0.8%

9. In 2015, the Philippines earned P227.6B from international tourism. Of this amount, the top visitor was South Korea at 29.2%. Then USA at 18.6%. China was only 4.5%. Not even close.

10. China is a clear top contributor in one aspect. The trade value of illegal drugs in the Philippines was estimated at $8.3B in 2013. 96% of this is shabu, sourced almost exclusively from China.

WHAT DO ALL THESE TELL US

1. Duterte's rants are not rooted on large-scale data but selective nitpicking & twisting of facts to fit his narrative.

2. US is our main economic partner now & in the future. Our competitive advantage (BPO) fits perfectly with their market. Runner-up is not even China, but Japan. Piss off the US, and its ally Japan, to get close to China - that's economic hara-kiri. This strategy of attack the West to appease the East is strategically flawed. We will lose more than our shoals. We will lose our main markets.

3. China leads in only one area - supplying illegal drugs to the country. Whatever donation China makes is dwarfed by the damage caused by

its drug syndicates. Materials for drug rehab will be peanuts compared to the billions siphoned off. Duterte should ask for the Chinese to ship him the Triad drug lords, not construction materials.

Duterte's gratitude to the Chinese, and hostility to the Americans are clearly misplaced.

oo00oo

5.

"The Taxman Cometh"
(But What Doth He Bringeth?)

Ruben Rivera
Dateline, Feb 27, 2005, 62ndForum Site

To what I've previously said about taxes, I would like to add the following:

1. THE INHERITANCE TAX - Typically, when the taxman cometh after the death of a pater/mater familias, the family have had to spend thousands of pesos for hospital & doctor bills, w/c might have practically impoverished a middle class family if the decedent had a months-long bout with cancer, some kidney disease, etc.; there might have been surgery, ICU stay, dialysis, & so forth. They then face the additional expenses for the funeral parlor, the wake, feeding of mourners, the burial (w/c might entail purchase of a plot in some "memorial park"). All the above expenses are "deductible" from the "estate," but what estate is there? In most cases, the estate, or the major portion of it, consists of a lot and house, plus maybe a vacant lot somewhere that was purchased "for the children." There may be 4 to 6 children, one or two of whom might still be in high school or college. If the house & lot are in Metro Manila, the taxman may insist that their value is say, P15 MILLION. To pay the estate tax, the property may have to be sold - so where will the family stay while looking for another place to live? The family

property may have sentimental value, etc. If it is sold, some of the children may want to have their share of the estate in cash, leaving the others w/o enough money to buy a dwelling place. If the decedent left a small "business," like say a motor repair shop, this might have to be sold - & a source of income might be lost to the family. The decedent might have had some money in the bank, but if this hasn't been used up for the above-mentioned expenses, the children would rightfully think - why should the gov't get a share of this hard-earned money, when after all Papa/Mama had been paying income taxes through all the years? Is it any wonder that there is so much resistance to the inheritance tax - that, as I've said, "the gorge rises up" among the heirs when the taxman cometh for it? In our society, it is an inhumane tax. Rich clans are barely touched by it, for the taxman usually finds that the family had set up corporations the shares of which had been transferred to the heirs, before the death of father/mother, in tax-free ways; there could be "foundations" & "trusts" that had put most of the estate behind barriers impenetrable by Mr. Taxman. The inheritance tax, in the Philippines, is not only an inhumane tax & a tax directly counter to our cultural grain; it is impracticable, unproductive, easy to avoid, almost entirely, by the knowledgeable or those well-advised by lawyers & accountants; it's a breeder of corruption of both tax collectors & the taxed. It is a gangrenous growth that must be cut off from our legal system. The government's heart was "in the right place" when it made life insurance proceeds exempt from taxes. Shouldn't the human instinct behind that move apply also to the estate? Be it remembered that on that estate, presumably, income taxes, real estate taxes, other direct or indirect taxes had been levied & presumably paid. Why shpuld death mean the accrual of more taxes, since death, after all, did not bring with it any increment in overall wealth?

2. CORPSES HELD IN BOND - The proposal of Mr. Purisima (truly a guy "most pure" - he's a bachelor) about the government being given a lien on cadavers, such that these won't be released to relatives until the inheritance tax has been paid is just plainly ridiculous & inhumane. (I've nothing against bachelors - I was one of those myself, in another lifetime; I wanted to mention his status because his not being a family man might have dimmed his perception of his proposal, such that he didn't realize that in making it, his "too, too solid flesh should have melted & turned into dew," to paraphrase somebody.)

Doesn't he know that in many - if not most - cases, even if the heirs are falling all over themselves in their eagerness to help the government thru payment of the estate tax, it wd. take time to determine what the estate is & its value, not to speak of the possible necessity to sell real property or a business so that the estate tax cd. be paid? In the meantime, ON THE VERY DAY OF THE DEATH, the immediate family, other relatives, and friends feel extremely obligated, out of affection or moral obligation, to get the body of Papa/Mama from the hospital, where it lies on a slab at a corner of the basement morgue. If it has to lie there, or in some refrigeration facility (w/c the hospital wd. have to build, if Purisima's proposal becomes law), won't the indignity inflicted on the dead person, the postponement of rites of mourning for & honoring of the deceased, & the accrual day to day of expenses for storage of the corpse, arouse deep hatred of & bitterness towards the government? Some families might not even have the wherewithal to pay the usual bills of hospital & doctors; now they're burdened too w/ having to IMMEDIATELY pay a tax, hateful in itself, to the government - for what? What service or benefit comes from the government, in the circumstances? If part of the estate has to be sold to raise money for the taxes, won't this make the delay last for months? What if there are disputes about the estate, including possibly claims of creditors? Since quite often the bereaved families wd. be poor, or just able to make a decent living for themselves, corpses may pile up in hospital morgues & then later in refrigeration facilities, & may never be claimed. Who then will pay the expenses that accrue daily? Would businessmen deem it worthwhile to invest in refrigeration centers for corpses held in bond? If not, then the government wd. have to set up, ALL OVER THE COUNTRY, these facilities, & in the end, in a lot of cases, wd. not be able to collect the estate tax anyway, or perhaps collect only an amount that wd. pay for the storage expenses for only a few days. Not only wd. the country end up poorer, it wd. be the laughing stock of the world. Well, that's one way that our "bayang magiliw" cd. gain some distinction - thru one of these Guiness-type books?

3. THE ACTUAL TAXES THAT "THE COMMON TAO" PAYS - I'd just like to expand a

little what I've already said about this. Let's consider the country's top corporation - San Miguel Corporation, & one of the products - canned corned beef - produced by one of its wholly-owned subsidiaries. How is that product priced? Of course much of the price covers actual costs of ingredients & the packaging material. But if we consider total production costs, there wd. be, aside from the taxes, such as custom duties, that I referred to in my previous posting, other taxes that wd. have to be covered by the price the consumer pays. The company pays real estate taxes - not only on land but also on buildings & equipment (not just production equipment but also office/factory airconditioning equipment & other kinds of non-production "fixed" equipment); taxes levied by the local government; garbage fees, license fees, & other kds. of governmental charges; SSS contributions; documentary stamp taxes passed on to it by banks, etc.; taxes on its bank accounts & bank transactions. Its employees, because of the sizeable withholding tax on their wages, demand higher wages, so that effectively the company pays practically all the income tax paid by its workers. There's even a tax on overseas telephone calls. Law firms, accounting firms, security firms, consultants, etc. servicing the company increase their charges because they have to pay tax, so effectively the company pay the taxes. Then of course the company pays income tax, which it considers an expense, and so the prices of all products cover part of this tax. All the taxes I referred to in my earlier e-mail, plus those mentioned here, ARE OF COURSE PASSED ON TO THE CONSUMER VIA THE PRICE for the can of corned beef. Can you imagine then, the amount of tax that the consumer effectively shells out to the government, when he/she buys that can of corned beef? The company trumpets that it contributes to government coffers billions of Pesos thru the income tax it pays - that SMC is the No. 1 taxpayer in the RP - but who really pays the taxes - including INCOME TAX - that supposedly the company paid, not to speak of the wage taxes, taxes of advertising firms, etc., passed on to the company, but reflected in the company's books not as taxes but as part of costs of "production" or of "marketing," or of "expenses" of some sort? Expensive "perks" of executives such as luxury cars for personal use, country club membership fees & free foreign travel (perhaps w/ spouse) are taxed as part of compensation, & of course these taxes ultimately find their way to the tag price of the can of corned beef. If we consider the other things that the "common tao" has to buy (including electricity, water supply, cooking gas), should we not say that in fact he pays a HEAVY TAX JUST FOR LIVING, even if his income is below the taxable level or he files no IT return (if he's an employee, in any case tax has probably been withheld from his wages & already remitted to the gov't)?

Another point. It is said that in the U.S. & Europe, a much bigger percentage of people who shd. pay taxes do pay taxes, as compared to the percentage of such people in the Philippines. But in the "advanced" countries, isn't it that much of the taxes paid go back to the people, in the form of services, amenities, & benefits given by the government? The return from the government is visible or palpable to the people. Does this happen too in the Philippines? If it doesn't - or if it doesn't happen commensurately - shouldn't we justly expect that the proportion here of the no. of people who pay taxes, to the no. of people obliged to pay taxes, wd. be much lesser than such proportion in those "advanced" countries?

ooO0Ooo

6.

The Davao Music Connection

Danny Gil

(Danny Gil is a retired mechanical engineer after working many years in USA. He finished at UP. Now he is busy with their farm in Tanjay, together with his wife, Lisa. He is a writer and author of Ramblings Book series that I published. I also published his mother Avelina Gil's books and his late columnist brother Gerry Gil's book. I also published his late aunt Soledad Juan's book of poems.)

Dateline, October 12, 2016, Ramblings File

Two years ago, there was an impromptu party at our house that lasted till 3 in the morning. A cousin of Lisa had passed away and his wake was at their house just across the street. Now, there was this excellent violinist visiting from Davao who played a piece or two at the wake. Lisa remembers Gary Inigo from the mid 1950s, as a 12 year old kid. He already was pretty good with the violin he inherited from his actor-musician dad, who died during the war, and since his mother was a niece to the parish priest, he grew up practically in the church. He eventually went off to Davao becoming an engineer, among others. Duterte still is one of his patrons who calls him often to perform music. At that time, he made a good musical duo with "ouido style" pianist, 16 year old Lina Bao. She went off to Manila to study music, then eventually moved to the US. And she was also at the wake. Now, 56 years later, they meet again in Tanjay, and felt they still could make good music together. It wasn't appropriate at the wake, so we invited them over (plus whoever else was in the wake) to our house where Lina could play piano to compliment Gary's violin. We stayed on till 3 in the morning, jamming, singing, reminiscing, debating, drinking, eating, etc. What made it so interesting is that Gary converted to Islam 15 years ago, and was most vocal about everything. With an engineer's mind, he could dissect, quote the bible and Koran, and make his points. His wife, Neneng, who almost became a nun, also converted. Most fascinating. Anyway, at one point, about 30 people from the wake came over and joined in the jamming, including Fr Jun, the son of the deceased, and another niece who brought her piccolo. See two left photos below.

The next day, we lent Lina our full keyboard Roland electric piano for the duration of her week's stay at the Pensione House, where she hosted a party for more old friends. We had more jamming.

See photo above. At that time, I made a video of these jammings and posted it on U-tube for Gary's computer savvy children. Here is the link:

https://www.youtube.com/watch?v=rUR4eUH9uDw

I gave Lina a Cdrom disk. I would be the first to recommend against playing it, because that is the first and last time I've attempted to hog the limelight and sing, all 14 minutes long, ugh. (At least it's only my voice at times, no video of me). I recently reviewed it and Gary reminds me of Fiddler On The Roof. And he also plays the piano/keyboard pretty well.

--oOo--

Over 2 months ago, Lisa and I were in Manila, and we got cheap tickets for Davao. Lisa never has been there and my last visit was over 40 years ago. We booked for 3 days and planned to do all the tourist trappings just by ourselves. Our main target was the Sul Orchid farm, then maybe 1 or 2 of the well advertised parks such as Eden.

The Davao bombing had just occurred and we figured it would make it maybe more exciting. We emailed Gary and mentioned about our visit, and he right away offered to take us around. Gary, Neneng and one of their sons met us at the airport, brought us to the hotel, then we all had lunch at the Mall nearby, then off they drove maybe 30 km to the Sul Orchard farm. That is us (above pic) posing at the farm with Neneng in Muslim outfit. More orchid photos on left below.

Lisa bought about a dozen of the more rare seedlings for our Tanjay farm, and these were carefully packed. Then, they proceeded to bring us back to the hotel with the promise that tomorrow, they bring us to Eden Park. On the way back, Gary decided to drop by Pres Duterte's house, and if the big man were around, Gary was certain we all could have an audience with him. The guards knew Gary, and after sign-in, waved us through.

But alas, Duterte was busy at a rally somewhere, and the best we could do was a group photo with his cardboard image. See photo above. The scheduled trip to Eden Park the next day didn't push through because of a glitch with the vehicle. Besides it was supposed to be just with Neneng with her son driving. Gary was performing at a wedding in the posh Marco Polo Hotel. So Lisa and I went off on our own to Malagos Nature Park via rental car.

It reminded us much of the Singapore Gardens we visited years ago, but this time, even if in much smaller scale, we got tired, and stayed just over 2 hours after a healthy organic lunch. See the photos shown.

 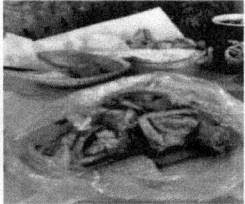

That evening, we were treated to dinner at Gary's house, and again came out the violin, keyboard, and jamming of us all. Early on, we had scratched off the other "must see" trappings of Davao such as the Pearl Farm as it required an over- night stay and was a bit pricey. Maybe on our next visit. We did some shopping at Barter Trade, had lunch at what turned out to be an expensive seafood restaurant that specialized in crabs, shrimps, lobsters. We over-ordered. See first dish below. But back in our Makati house, we had occasion for more parties such as for my visiting US-based brother, some cousins, and my Ma, who is 99.

See photos.

And finally, Lisa's 75th birthday. We flew home to Tanjay the next day.

ooOOoo

7.

Duterte's Mindset

Roger Reyes (Ogie)

Dateline, October 12, 2016, Cepol Yahoogroup, via email

Bay Martin, thanks. What a relief!

It must have been very difficult for you, a fellow Mindanao-anon, to take with a nonchalant stride or even in jest, Du30's mind set that propelled all the uncalled for insecurities of the Filipinos and our allies, leaving everyone guessing when his mind would become stable and sensible and what will become of our beloved Philippines.

The same day that the USA short-ended the joint RP-US Military exercise by one day, FVR, the only big shot Du30 named [but not shamed, hehehe...] who came to him to convince him to run, made an extraordinary effort to **go public** with his wish for **Du30 to shape up for a "21st century** [and beyond] thinking, acting and living" with a well-studied balanced 20/20 futuristic eyesight and leave his problematic 20th century mind set for good.

It was a shock to Du30 and all his pencil pushers, ardent insiders who are forced to treat him as a demigod for money and selfish opportunism's sake, hehe, and "EJK thrilled" fans to hear from FVR, our envoy to China, what Du30 was doing to himself in coercing his people to live in the past, particularly those best forgotten as mere historical events, ought to be taken best as stepping stones toward a progressive Filipino country living peacefully in harmony with the rest of the 195 nations in the world, who together with an interdependent foreign policy have learned that the best way to live is to stay connected and helping each other, acting as one in an diverse but interdependent world.

FVR is hopeful that Du30 at his age he can still change if he desires to hit the ground running with a very well studied master plan to change himself. But it will be a long challenging hard work. It is not easy for him to metamorphose FROM a primitive leader living alone in Davao City away from the center of civilization and doing well TO a modern leader of his nation that understands how the 21st century and beyond should be lived and LED.

How far behind in time is his mind set? You will not be surprised with the DDS, are other examples: two of my teen grandnephews living in Davao City visited us a week ago and told us in reference to his non-stop attack against De Lima, "That's how he treats his enemies. Sus, lolo, you should hear how the radios, papers and tv "blared" with daily attacks against Nograles when he ran against Du30. He won't stop." On another teenage concern, the racing champ grandnephew, lamented, "Imagine lolo, 30 kmh among speed limit!!" With the social media and the net, kids know how the modern world is lived and how enemies are best treated. Their common comment, "He does not listen to anybody."

Don't despair, there is still hope for Du30 and the finest start he can make is by listening to the majority of the voters who DIDN'T vote for his election, Their number is around 26M compared to 16M who voted for him. What of the entire population? His fans will take seriously the polls who say the people trust him. BUT, they forgot the 26M voters who didn't cast their votes for him!!! whose figure is more **determining** or **convincing** than the polls that we don't how they are done and representing only the usual 1,200 respondents of a population of 102M! What a few number to study and represent 42M voters and to the 102M population!

The change should not only be in the mindset, but also the way he talks using his body language. You know when he talks serious, he looks like he is the old Tatay with a traditional angry disciplining look and tightly gripping a belt on one hand; when he is angry he looks like he is already punishing and you feel the blows. When he jokes or smiles, the way he has been, you can't get the feeling that he is only flattering or fooling you. Well, I have to be honest, that is ONLY how my family and acquaintances see him. I don't claim that he looks that way to others. NOT to his close in-crowd and his cabinet secretaries. Oh, yes, when he holds his press con after midnight to early dawn people are sleeping and not listening to him. What a way to avoid contact with the people!.

Du30 must know his timing. Oh, the press cons?? Maybe he does, come to think of it, when he lambasted Obama who is deep in campaigning for his party's candidate Hillary Clinton whom the enemy Russia is seen as supporting her opponent

Trump. He lambasts the USA and lauds Russia that he admires and wants to replace the USA as his big brother. Gosh, you can't do that in an election period! Surely, if done, it will only be for spite, in revenge for Obama's fatherly advise on his EJK. Certainly, Obama will not like it and I believe is already hitting back with his first salvos of cutting short the military exercise and setting up a most influential pro-USA ex-president FVR to take a bash at him.

We'll see how our efforts to make him a better president will go. It will be a lot more fun now that many have expressed their constitutional right to open their mouths or found the courage to liberate themselves from Du30's EJK highly contagious and "still" mass appealing strategy.

Hoping for the best.

ooO0Ooo

8.

Dissing God, Cussing Obama and Praising Hitler - What a Week

Rodel Rodis

Dateline, Oct. 7, 2016, published at: www. globalnation.inquirer.net, usp4gg@yahoogroups. com, globalfildiaspora@yahoogroups.com, ateneof orbetterphilippines@yahoogroups.com, Filipino-American_Network@yahoogroups.com, all@naffaa.org and 2 more...

President Duterte's mouth set a new world record for traveling the longest distance in the shortest time. In a span of just six days, it traveled from doubting God in Heaven to condemning Obama to Hell and they were not even the most offensive remarks uttered in that week.

Speaking before journalists in Malacanang Palace on September 27, 2016, Duterte justified the restoration of the death penalty as necessary to "make up for divine inconsistency". (*"Duterte: I can teach God about justice"*). In his speech, Duterte criticized the "bleeding hearts" in the Catholic

Church for their opposition to the death penalty because of their belief that "only God can kill". Duterte said he did not want to have to wait until Judgment Day. "What if there is no God?" he asked.

Six days later, in an October 3 speech to local officials, Duterte complained that the United States was refusing to sell weapons to his government and, therefore, President Obama "can go to hell." He had been angered by Washington's criticism of his take-no-prisoners crusade against drug addicts and he threatened to turn to China and Russia for weapons purchases.

Duterte may not realize that the funds used by the Philippines to purchase weapons from the US come from US military assistance ($340 million since 2001) and they can only be used to purchase US arms, not arms from Russia or China.

THE LEAHY LAW

Contrary to Duterte's assumption, Pres. Obama's refusal to authorize the Philippine purchase of US arms was not to get back at him for his "son of a whore" insult, but to comply with the Leahy Law, named after principal sponsor Sen. Patrick Leahy of Vermont, which prohibits the U.S. Department of State and Department of Defense from providing military assistance to foreign military units that violate human rights with impunity.

In the same week that Duterte had cussed Obama, Sen. Leahy denounced Duterte on the floor of the US Senate for "advocating and endorsing what amounts to mass murder." Sen. Ben Cardin of Maryland echoed Leahy's sentiment: "Senator Leahy is absolutely right when he said that a lack of respect for rule of law and democratic governance breeds instability, distrust, and sometimes violence."

Obama has no choice but to comply with the "rule of law", the Leahy Law, a problem that doesn't exist for the despots in Russia or China.

There is a way to get around the Leahy Law, as US Major General Paul Eaton explained: "The value of the Leahy Law is that it serves as a moral guide to the application of U.S. military engagement. Some in the U.S. armed forces have argued that the law frustrates U.S. partnership at precisely the moment we need most to influence better behaviors. This dilemma has a solution embedded in the amendment itself, which provides that if human rights remediation has begun, U.S. assistance can be brought to bear."

Unfortunately, human rights "remediation" is not likely to happen any time soon under Duterte. In fact, it may only get exponentially worse.

"HAPPY TO SLAUGHTER THEM"

On September 30, after arriving back in Manila from a brief official visit to Vietnam, Duterte complained that he had been "portrayed or pictured to be a cousin of Hitler."

Rather than objecting to it, Duterte reveled in the comparison. "Hitler massacred 3 million Jews ... there's 3 million drug addicts," he said. "There are. I'd be happy to slaughter them."

Duterte's newly appointed Philippine Ambassador to the United Nations, Teddyboy Locsin, Jr, posted a tweet in support of his boss: "I believe that the Drug Menace is so big it needs a FINAL SOLUTION like the Nazis adopted. That I believe. NO REHAB."

The pushback was immediate. German Foreign Ministry spokesman Martin Schaefer denounced Duterte's comments as "unacceptable" stating: "It is impossible to make any comparison to the unique atrocities of the Shoah and Holocaust."

World Jewish Congress President Ronald Lauder said Duterte's remarks were "revolting" and added: "Drug abuse is a serious issue. But what President Duterte said is not only profoundly inhumane, but it demonstrates an appalling disrespect for human life that is truly heartbreaking for the democratically elected leader of a great country."

Rep. Teodoro Baguilat asked Duterte if his policy means that "it's open season now for all addicts, no more rehabilitation, just kill them systematically like what the Nazis did with the Jews."

Duterte was not content to just happily slaughter 3 million drug addicts in the Philippines, he even sought to export his kill-the-drug-addicts policy to Indonesia.

After he attended the ASEAN conference in Laos, Duterte visited Indonesia where the country's anti-drugs chief, Budi Waseso, held a press conference declaring that Indonesia would launch a Duterte-style drug purge. Later, however, a spokesman for the national narcotics agency clarified that Indonesian "punishments have to be in accordance with our law and with national and international standards."

REHABILITATION FOR DRUG ADDICTS

Indonesia is evaluating its treatment of drug addicts. In an article in The Jakarta Post on March 20, 2014 ("Should drug addicts be jailed or rehabilitated?"), Kartono Mohamad, the chairman of the Indonesian Public Health Scholars Association, wrote that "the idea of treating drug users as criminals came from the fact they use or are in possession of drugs, which by law are declared illegal...On the other hand, drug addiction is also considered a form of social disease, like prostitution. Not so long ago HIV was also regarded a social disease. That is why Law No. 35/2009 on narcotics and addictive drugs provides treatment and rehabilitation for drug addicts, but not for drug traffickers or dealers."

"In that case, we are inclined to differentiate between those who intentionally hook other people to become addicts and those who are the victim of the former group. Here starts the idea of treating drug addicts as victims. As victims they deserve empathy, treatment and assistance to get rid of their addiction through rehabilitation."

The same reevaluation of the treatment of drug addicts is taking place in the United Arab Emirates where Sheikh Saif bin Zayed, the Minister of Interior and Deputy Prime Minister, had ordered all concerned authorities to evaluate current anti-drugs laws and suggest reforms.

Brig Gen Maktoum al Sharifi, the head of the Abu Dhabi Capital Police, welcomed the idea of reforms, saying the law should not consider a drug offender a criminal, as it currently does.

"A drug addict is a sick person and he should be treated as such," Brig Gen al Sharifi said. "Alternative punishment would be more effective. A drug offender could be just an addict, not a criminal, but after locking him up for years he could come out involved in crimes such as stealing, drug dealing, et cetera." The Abu Dhabi Police has proposed alternative punishments which include community service, such as cleaning the streets, schools or voluntary work.

"I WILL KILL THREE MILLION"

To cap a strange week, Duterte visited a Jewish Synagogue in Manila on Sunday October 2 to apologize to the Jewish people for his remarks. In a speech that was televised nationally, he explained that his comments were a reaction to negative criticism. "So I said, 'Sure, I am Hitler, but the ones I will kill are these drug addicts ... but it is not really that I said something wrong. But rather, they do not really want to tinker with the memory so I apologize profoundly and deeply to the Jewish people."

http://www.dw.com/en/philippine-president-duterte-apologizes-for-pro-hitler-comments/a-35943457

"I would like to make it clear, here and now, that there was never an intention on my part to derogate the memory of six million Jews murdered. The reference to me was, I was supposedly Hitler, who killed many people ... But I was very emphatic. I will kill three million," he said.

And then he unloaded again:: "The Americans, I don't like them ... they are reprimanding me in public. So I say: 'Screw you, f--k you, everything else. You are stupid."

And that's how President Duterte ended his week.

(Send comments to Rodel50@gmail.com or mail them to the Law Offices of Rodel Rodis at 2429 Ocean Avenue, San Francisco, CA 94127).

Photos, courtesy of Inquirer.Net

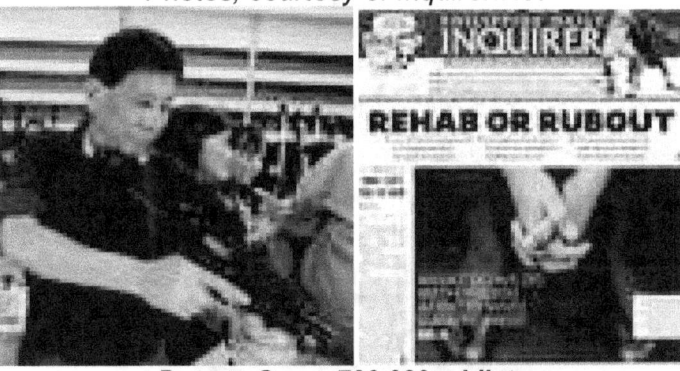

Duterte Gun + 700,000 addicts

Duterte-China + Grieving wife

Danica May Garcia

ooO0Ooo

9.

Burning bridges?
That Does It.

Korina Sanchez
(The Freeman)

A well-known TV Host and Media person in the
Philippines

Dateline, October 10, 2016

Reports have it that the Americans have
pulled out some of its remaining equipment left
over in Zamboanga from a mission that ended last
April of 2015. These include transport vehicles. The
Americans probably just left them in case they are
needed, since the country and the US have several
agreements regarding military exercises and the
like.But last Tuesday, a C-17 Globemaster cargo
plane landed in Zamboanga, and loaded the
equipment. There was no comment from the
Western Mindanao Command, nor a statement
from the US Embassy as to the pullout of the

vehicles. Right there, you can opine for yourself as to why.

President Duterte has made known his disdain, even hate for the Americans in the past 100 days he has been in office. He said he wanted the Americans out of Mindanao, then the whole country. He said that this year's war games would be the last. He said that he would review the EDCA and probably other existing agreements with regards to American military presence in the country. He officially informed the US that the country will not participate in joint patrols of the South China Sea. He has also repeatedly cursed, hurled invectives at the US and the EU, including President Obama, and dared them to stop whatever aid they were giving the country, adding that if America was not with us, they are against us.

According to the Duterte administration, America has failed the country, and that the country has not really benefitted from the long-standing friendship with the US. All this, while cozying up to China, and even Russia. Duterte will visit China this October. The way I see it, he has effectively greased up the Chinese to be in their good graces, which he has made publicly clear. Time to seek out new friends, while all but dumping old ones. When one curses at a friend, and mind you, not in the seemingly harmless way a Filipino does in some conversations that strain the relationship.

Despite all the statements from the US, the UN and the EU that the relationship is still strong, being constantly pushed out the door will eventually have an effect. Duterte will pitch the country to the Chinese, and will also ask for developmental aid, such as that railway he has always wanted. He also hopes to get China to allow Filipino fishermen to return to Panatag Shoal, which is occupied by several Chinese vessels that prevent anyone else from fishing.

The fact that Duterte has to even ask the Chinese it only highlights that the Permanent Court of Arbitration ruling in favor of the country has no power at all. They do not want the Chinese to "lose face" as one government official puts it when the PCA arbitration was mentioned. Obviously, everything is being done to please the Chinese. How all this plays out for the country remains to be seen. I have mentioned that we are now sailing in uncharted waters. I will admit that we have been used to almost everything American all these years, and that change may at first be difficult. As it is, the Duterte administration may be burning an important bridge, in the hope of building a new, albeit untested one.

oo0Ooo

10.

A Nation in Pain

Perry Diaz

Dateline, Oct. 11, 2016, PerryScope

Jennilyn Olayres weeping over the body of her husband, Michael Siaron, who was killed in the Manila metropolitan area. (Reuters)

A Social Weather Stations (SWS) survey conducted last September 24-26 showed Duterte receiving a public satisfaction rating of 76%, "dissatisfied" rating of 11%, and "undecided" rating of 13%. According to SWS, Duterte's +54 "net satisfaction" rating is better than most of his post-EDSA revolution predecessors, except for Fidel V. Ramos who scored +66 in 1992.

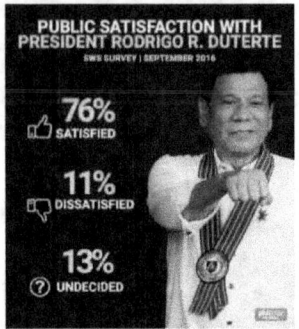

During that same period last September, the SWS survey showed that 84% of the respondents are satisfied with the ongoing campaign against illegal drugs, while 8% are dissatisfied and 8% are undecided. The question asked was: "Please tell me how satisfied or dissatisfied you are with the performance of government in its campaign against illegal drugs?"

What SWS survey reveals?

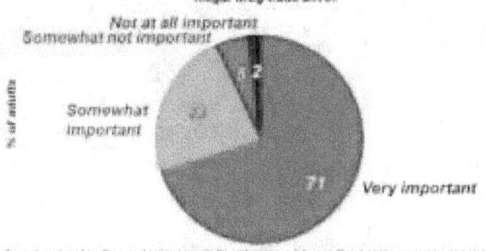

But here is the stinger: 94% of the respondents believed the importance of keeping the drug suspects alive during police operations. Only 6% believed that it was not important. The question asked was: "In the police's fulfillment of their duty in the campaign against illegal drugs, in your opinion, how important is it that they arrest suspects allegedly involved in the illegal drug trade alive?"

Is it then fair to presume that the respondents believed that killing the drug suspects should be avoided and that the police shouldn't be trigger-happy when arresting drug suspects?

It brings to fore the question: Are the police trained to avoid killing the drug suspects whenever possible? Or, is Duterte's "shoot to kill" order encouraging the police officers to use their guns as a "first resort" instead of "last resort."

"Shoot first..."

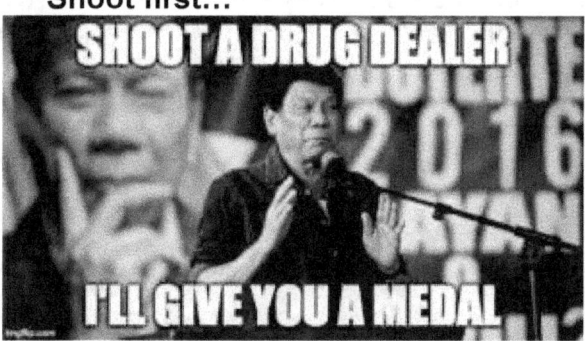

This brings to mind a cliché that's used in police operations, to wit: "Shoot first, ask questions later." Although no police department would openly encourage its policemen to shoot first and ask questions later, there is a culture within the law enforcement community that a policeman should always be ready to shoot first and ask questions later. Their mindset is: It's either they shoot first or they're dead.

However, the "Shoot first, ask questions later" mantra is predicated on a situation where shots weren't meant to kill but merely wound the target so that the police could question him later. But what has been happening is oftentimes the target ends up dead because the police use high-caliber weapons... and at short range. In other words, it's not "Shoot first, ask questions later" but "Shoot to kill." But isn't that in line with what Duterte wants, which is to kill drug pushers and drug addicts? Didn't he say during the campaign, "All of you who are into drugs, you sons of bitches, I will really kill you"? Didn't he offer medals and cash rewards to citizens who killed drug dealers? And few weeks after his oath-taking as president, didn't he reiterate his vow during his inaugural State of the Nation Address (SONA), saying: ""We will not stop until the last drug lord ... and the last pusher have surrendered or are put either behind bars or below the ground, if they so wish"?

Terror effect

Two days before Duterte took his oath, more than 3,000 self-confessed drug pushers

and users in South Cotobato and Sultan Kudarat surrendered.

After reaching Duterte's 100th day in office, Communications Secretary Martin Andanar announced in a press conference: *"It's a complete success and the people believe in it. 84% believe in the war against illegal drugs. 700,000 addicts turned themselves in kasama ang (including) 52,000 na drug pushers and drug lords."* He added: *"You see crime dropping. Last July, it dropped at 49%. I don't have it in front of me but I have new data from January to September, crime dropped to about 40 percent."*

While the drop in crime may be attributed to "terror effect" — which was intended against the drug syndicates — it is also terrorizing communities throughout the countries. Citizens are afraid to go out at night lest they be mistaken for drug pushers or users and killed by the police or vigilantes... or people who have an axe to grind against them.

Dutertismo

Former President Fidel V. Ramos confers with President Rodrigo Duterte at the start of the new administration.

In the long run, extra-judicial killings (EJKs) — or "salvaging," a Marcos martial law-era jargon — and other indiscriminate killings would corrode the base of "Dutertismo," a movement based on mass support for Duterte's leadership in fighting corruption, crime, poverty, and other social problems. But, just like similar events in the history of mankind, there is a caveat here. Abuse of power and the impunity of corruption could turn that "mass support" into "mass protest," which could mimic the people power revolutions of the past.

It's interesting to note that one of Duterte's early and ardent supporters – former President Fidel V. Ramos – wrote in his newspaper column: *"In the overall assessment by this writer [Ramos], we find our Team Philippines losing in the first 100 days of Du30's [Duterte] administration – and losing badly. This is a huge disappointment and letdown to many of us."*

"Death under investigation"

"Death under Investigation"

Last September when the SWS survey was taken, the Philippine National Police (PNP) said that 1,011 drug pushers and users were killed from July 1 to September 4. In addition, there were 1,391 deaths considered as "death under investigation" (DUI) or those whose bodies were found with cardboards with the note *"Pusher ako"* (I am a pusher). A month later, the DUIs have increased to 1,745 cases; however, only 321 cases have been filed against the alleged perpetrators – vigilantes? — of the crime, of which 176 cases were considered solved. However, "solved" in PNP parlance doesn't mean the perpetrator has been convicted; it merely means that an arrest has been made.

During a media interview, PNP Director General Ronald "Bato" dela Rosa attributed the deaths of suspected drug pushers to illegal drug syndicates purging their own ranks or due to turf wars or double-crosses in drug transactions. "You will be surprised, this is not the handiwork of vigilantes. These alleged vigilante killings, it turned out, are syndicated killings."

But whether the EJKs were perpetrated by drug syndicates, vigilantes or the police, it is causing international furor because EJKs are considered human rights violations. In particular, U.S. President Barack Obama was concerned about the impunity of EJKs in the Philippines. This did not dwell too well with Duterte, who told Obama, "Go to hell."

The people's "message"

"Stop the killings!"

The Philippines has been getting military and police financial assistance for many years from the U.S. The military receives at least $200 million a year, of which part of it is used in law enforcement. The U.S. military assistance is in jeopardy or it could be terminated to ensure that it will not be used for EJK operations. A U.S. State Department spokesman explained, *"There's a law called the Leahy Law that requires us to routinely and regularly vet security forces that are getting aid and assistance to make sure that any units that violate international law in that regard do not get aid and assistance."*

Indeed, with all the brouhaha over his controversial "War on Drugs," Duterte has become an international pariah. Recently, a French daily newspaper, *"The Liberation,"* in a front-page article, Duterte was described as a "serial killer president." The four-page story also touched on Duterte's expletives against Obama and Pope Francis, and his controversial remarks in which he compared Adolf Hitler's extermination of Jews to his "war on drugs."

At the end of the day, the "message" from the SWS survey last September is crystal clear: While they want Duterte to stop the drug menace, they want him to do it in a way where killings are avoided. "Stop the killings!" was what the people were saying.

The Filipino people are an extraordinary kind of people. They can tolerate the evils of corruption and endure the pains of poverty. But they are too forgiving of others' transgressions. And to the Filipino psyche, killing is never an option.

But in the final analysis, when our nation is in pain, there is only one option and that is, we turn to God – we say, *"Bahala Na."*

ooO0oo

11.

Appeal For The First and Foremost Step in Poverty Reduction: Progressive Taxation

Marcelo Tecson

(A CPA and Concerned Citizen, C/o San Juan and Associates, 27S Midland Manor 2, Ortigas Avenue Greenhills, San Juan City 1500)

Dateline, Oct. 14, 2016

JUST WHY ARE WE HELPLESS IN MINIMIZING THE GLOBALLY LAMENTED PROBLEM OF LACK OF INCLUSIVE GROWTH, GROSS WEALTH AND INCOME INEQUALITY, OR THE RICH GETTING RICHER AND THE POOR POORER?

IF THERE IS A PROBLEM, IT IS MAN-MADE—IT IS THE LACK OF POLITICAL WILL OF GOVERNMENTS IN INSTITUTING THE LEGAL, MORAL, EQUITABLE, AND EXPEDITIOUS WAY OF DOING IT: PROGRESSIVE TAXATION

WHICH EQUATES TO GIVING THE POOR ENOUGH FOR THEIR BASIC NECESSITY, AND LEAVING THE RICH ENOUGH FOR THEIR LUXURY—WHO WILL ARGUE AGAINST THAT?

WE CAN WAIT 'TIL KINGDOM COME BUT THE RICH WILL NOT VOLUNTARILY SHARE THEIR SURPLUS WEALTH (SOME PROBABLY DERIVED FROM THEIR OVER-PRICED GOODS AND SERVICES) TO THE POOR ON A SUSTAINED BASIS; THUS, THERE IS NO ALTERNATIVE TO HAVING THE RICH COMPULSORILY DO IT THROUGH PROGRESSIVE TAXATION, WHICH ENTAILS TAKING SOME MORE FROM THE ABUNDANT ANNUAL INCOME OF THE RICH (BUT NOT FROM THEIR EXISTING WEALTH) AND SPENDING FOR THE POOR'S POVERTY REDUCTION THE BADLY NEEDED INCREASE IN TAX COLLECTION.

For: All GOVERNMENT OFFICIALS
Concerned

Subject: DOF-proposed progressive
taxation is not progressive enough

The media-reported revised individual income tax brackets and rates, for endorsement to Congress by the Department of Finance (DOF), is a great stride towards the constitutionally-mandated PROGRESSIVE TAXATION, under which the RICH who can pay more taxes are constrained to pay more, and those who can pay less are allowed to pay less. Indeed, this should be the case because compared to the POOR, the

RICH have to pay a PREMIUM for the perpetuation of what they currently enjoy—great wealth and luxurious lifestyle.

PROGRESSIVE TAXATION is DOABLE because its implementation does not require huge precious public funds.

However, the DOF-proposed set of tax reforms is not progressive enough. Under it, while the RICH with their surplus wealth can still enjoy their luxurious lifestyle, millions of already miserable JOBLESS Filipinos—who are without taxable income and will not benefit at all from income-tax-rate reduction—will be made more miserable by further INFLATIONARY consumption tax designed to recover the proposed income tax reduction, thereby making the POOR even POORER!

As presented in the enclosed paper on recommended PROGRESSIVE TAXATION, a closer look into the DOF-proposed individual income tax reforms will show that the increase in top individual income tax rate for the ultra RICH—from 32% to 35%, or by a relatively small three percentage points—is not high enough, thereby constraining DOF to propose consumption taxation, something quite hard on JOBLESS Filipinos.

Why the Proposed Increase in Top Income Tax Rate is Not High Enough?

Together with the MIDDLE CLASS, the RICH will also benefit from reduced tax rates on their first P5,000,000 taxable income. Their additional income in excess of P5,000,000 up to P13,750,000 will be used merely for the recovery of their tax savings on their first P5,000,000 taxable income. It is only beyond their P13,750,000 income—seems very high and with few taxpayers covered—that the RICH will incur increased income tax due at the measly three-percentage point increment.

Hence, the top income tax bracket for the RICH should be raised to at least 40%, to avoid more INFLATIONARY consumption tax that is so hard and confiscatory on the POOR.

(Does it really take those who have suffered--or are still suffering--to understand and be kind to the suffering POOR, the bulk of our population? Is populism wrong? Doesn't our Constitution provide for majority rule, or the most number of votes in election, which equates to the greatest good for the greatest number--or what else if not constitutional populism--which should be done for as long as it is feasible? PROGRESSIVE TAXATION is feasible, or doable, because it is definitely beneficial and acceptable to the majority, and it does not need huge amount of scarce public funds in its implementation.)

Please note also the strongly recommended two-tier corporate income taxation, presented in my earlier emails.

For your attention and consideration.

Sincerely,

MARCELO L. TECSON

A CPA and Concerned Citizen

Cc, through separate letters/emails:

Senate President Koko Pimentel

Speaker Pantaleon Alvarez

Other executive and legislative government officials

Select members of media, academe, and economic society

Select civil society groups and concerned citizens, etc.

oo0Ooo

12.

Hindi Ko Akalain
(Never Expected This)

Jonathan Edwards J. Olabre

(Chief Fun Officer at <u>Stark Industries</u> - Schools attended - Ama Computer College, Computer Science and Pio Del Pilar Educ. Instituion + Lives in Pasig City)

Dateline, October 13, 2016, via Social Media

Hindi Ko Akalain.

It finally happened. Last night at around 7:00 PM, I have just finished dressing up. It was just to join school batchmates who were having a game of darts at the usual hangout. I was delayed from going out earlier since there was a thunderstorm. I had to take a bath and change clothes because I was caught in the rain on my way home. As I was picking up my things to bring, there were a series of loud raps on my door. As I opened it, there were 2 barangay tanods and 4 policemen. "28 B ba ito?" asked the tanod, I answered yes. I asked them who they were looking for, they did not answer but replied with "28 B ba ito?" I said yes again. Then they started looking furtively on all sides. I personally know the 2 tanod. And they also knew me. Then they retreated a few paces. I asked them again who were they looking for. No answer, then I told them if they needed anything. I told them that all the houses along this side are all numbered 28. They asked about 28 A, I told them where it is and I also told them that a city official lives there. Then they went away. I also went out and I saw them again. I asked again that if they needed anything from me since I am about to leave. They told me no, I was not needed.

I left but I no longer played darts. Between the laughing and the jokes and the ribbing from my batchmates that night, I was thinking. Was there Oplan Tokhang at night? The games ended and I went home. The morning after I was told that what happened was a mistake. There was a tip received yesterday that there was somebody taking shabu at an address and my address 28 B was given. It turned out that there was a mistake. It should have been 26 B.

Then it dawned on me. It was not Oplan Tokhang after all. It was a raid and my address was on the tip given by someone. It was a mistake but then the rage of all the things that transpired welled up in me. The thought of being a mistake, a collateral damage leaped from the newspaper headlines and right into my consciousness. It was me. I felt chills run up my spine and at the same time felt outrage. The cold arms of Death was wrapped around my shoulders the night before. They thought I was sniffing shabu. They received an unconfirmed tip that I was a drug addict. They went to my house, my house to see if I was sniffing shabu. Salpicas de mierda! Verdamt!

Only the 2 tanods saved me. They did not exactly say it but they recognized me. They know me. Then they realized that it was a mistake. It was that close! I was almost No. 3,001 on this days of terror. It was just a difference of 2 in that tipped off address. What if I had gone earlier? Would have they waited for me to go into that tipped off address and then what? What if it was a different tanod who accompanied the police? The vagaries of fate is what makes the difference then.

I ask my friends now who voted for Duterte. What would they say if the worst happened to me? "Jonathan was just collateral damage." "Oh it was a tragedy." Worse is "ah Jonathan used shabu. That is why he was so against Duterte." But you know me guys, I never touched the stuff.

The war has reached my front door. It is a war between good and evil. It is a war between civilization and barbarism. It is a war for our national soul. I just wonder when their eyes will open. Will I be just one of the casualties of this war?

I told a good friend about this earlier. She told me that I should keep quiet for the meantime with regards to my anti-Duterte posts. Ngayon pa ba ako tatahimik? I will not shut up. I will heighten my resistance. Writing this is part of that resistance. I will not be cowed. I will not be afraid because I am already terrified. Terrified on what has become of us. It was not like this a year ago. We have fought and won freedom 30 years ago. We defeated oppression 30 years ago. The War

On Drugs is no longer abstract for me. I never knew we would come to this pass. Hindi Ko Akalain.

There is a storm coming and it is a storm that nobody has ever seen.

"A poet must also know how to lead an attack." – Ho Chi Minh

ooOOoo

13.

Business Forecast, Etc.

Roger (Ogie) Reyes

Dateline, Oct. 13, 206

Look at this forecast by PSEi for the rest of the year until 2017 and up to 2020 and tell us what it means to you and our country and what we can do to offset our losses?
http://www.tradingeconomics.com/philippines/stock-market/forecast

Philippines Stock Market (PSEi) Forecast 2016-2020

The Philippines Stock Market (PSEi) is expected to trade at 7610.00 points by the end of this quarter, according...

Philippines Markets	Last	Q4/16	Q1/17	Q2/17	Q3/17	2020
Currency	48.5	48.62	49.1	49.58	50.07	57.77
Stock Market	7430	7610	7530	7460	7380	6150
Government Bond 10y	3.83	3.69	3.72	3.76	3.8	4.38

What is really happening? Is Du30 responsible? Or, someone, something else?

Sen. Ping Lacson said, ***"It is possibly Du30's mouth's fault."*** I'll be damned!

The chart shows that in just ONE year of Du30 our Peso is expected to drop to P50.07 to the USD. I think it is not Duterte's doing because his drug war and what follows immediately *[if he is worth believing, hehe, despite his usual "do this, ah.. that, er, go back to this..."]* **policy - the corruption war; both are "painstakingly designed" as he aggressively hit the ground running in July** *[amazing!, eh, could not be his, but the Manual's knowledgeable author]* **to make our RP "investment attractive."** But he could be wrong because he does not know much yet on how world economies work *[even unaware of his very own country's status & history, and people's Christian HR attitudes]* and unable to comprehend whether the wacky market's performance have anything to do with his **vile mouth** and **extra loud unnecessary accusations** against our allies and even the UN or whatever?

Perhaps the guy [could be *the now very much alarmed FVR who probably is thinking and realized that he had unleashed a monster*] or **some foreign organization** *[the CIA & reds can never be discounted]* **who gave Du30 his campaign funds and Governance Manual had predicted this decline due to the fact that the regulars see not much hope in us** *[under the sure election winner - him!]* **and instinctively felt convinced to venture to other markets for a better deal for their greed money's sake. To counter this, his Manual suggests that he try beguiling** *[baiting]* **money rich China into investing in RP to help us**

develop our industrial might in order to make his term full of hopes and investment attractive, *thereby keeping his hopes alive for leaving an unprecedented legacy!* China could take the opportunity to strengthen her bully-grabbed defensive shoals in our EEZ. *It would be a big take for China's health and hegemonic plans! Susmaryahosep, talaga! At redeeming kasi siya ang nagsusupply ng illegal drugas sa ating bayan.*

It's possible that the plunge would be the World Economy's doing if we get to ask the authors of "Economics for Dummies." From them we may get the cold sarcastic answer - *"It's the world economy, stupid, so start thinking and move your butts quickly! With or without regards to your 20th century wild man Du30 who's lost in the 21st century* [the last sentence is a courtesy of his "balimbing" supporter FVR]."

In case Du30 fails to beguile China and our economy really goes down to the dogs, we need not worry because we have a convenient fall guy in HIS person. Swerteee! Ayeeee... pero napakasakit po sa tao at sa ating mahal na bayan!

I hope the author of Du30 and his Manual, A guide to Governance, really knows what he has written - *the best advice under the circumstances and predicted future prevailing environment to every step Du30 takes in his 6 year term.* I say this because left alone to govern by himself and his know nothing waiter rah-rah boys, he cannot be able to overcome his deficiencies in personal talent and skills in time to know exactly what is happening and what he must do to meet the difficult and surprising challenges of his governance that he never met before in his little Davao City.

At this juncture, somehow I feel coerced to remember Sen. Ping Lacson's *[oh, there he is again!]* very concerned candidate voicing an ominous warning during the last campaign. He said, ***"If Du30 is elected God help us!"*** I believe he is now ardently admonishing us with, ***"Now see the chart, believe and do something for your survival or else!"***

Ok, no other choice for *[helpless???]* Christian RP but say lots and lots of prayers, ending with **"God please, please, please help us from this psychopath** *[courtesy of Agot]* **and lunatic** *[courtesy of Sen. Trillanes]* **monster!"**

Ogie and family, crossing their fingers with fears and tears but continue to write and plead.

ooO0Ooo

14.

Consider this my apology for being a Duterte supporter...

By Adrian

Dateline, Oct. 12, posted in some groups

https://www.reddit.com/r/Philippines/comments/54v sx4/consider_thi\s_my_apology_letter_for_being_a/ ?st=iu6i5pbf&sh

Consider this my apology letter for being a Duterte supporter during the election (self. Philippines) submitted 13 days ago by [deleted] Para sa mga kaibigan kong naniniwalang tama pa rin ang ginagawa ni Duterte: Gusto ko lang malaman mo na hindi ka nagiisa, ako din supporter nia dati. Naniwala dati sa mga pangako nia. Naniwala na baka sia na ang sagot sa madaming sakit ng mahal kong Pilipinas.

Pero tingnan mo ang ginawa ni Duterte ng manalo sia. Sino ang kinuha niang gabinete? Puro mga kaibigan at trapo. Yung tax reform na sinasabi nia, babawasan nga ang income tax pero ililipat din sa ibang bagay tulad ng gasolina, tatanggalin pa yung discount ng mga senior sa restaurant.

Yung mga drug matirx nia, puro palpak, kinailangan pa niang mag sorry. Yung war on drugs nia, ilang beses nang nadebunk ng reputable sources.

Pwede ko pa yan patawarin lahat, pero ang di ko matanggap ay pinapabagsak nia ang ekonomiya at tinatakot ang mga nagbibigay satin ng trabaho. May kaibigan ka ba o kakilala sa call center? Marunong ba silang mag intsik o russian? Pag umalis ba ang mga call center dito, magkakatrabaho ba sila?

At ang pinakapangit dito, ano ang punot dulong dahilan kung bakit kailangan niang magsalita ng di maganda? Dahil hindi sia marunong tumanggap ng kritisismo. Isipin mo, napuna lang sia ng mga westerners, hindi naman pabastos ang pagkakasabi sa kanya, pero ang laki laki na ng himutok ng butchi nia. Ganyan ba sia talaga? Konting kibot nagwawala sia? Ganyan ba dapat ang presidente? May mga ginagawa din namang tama si Duterte, pero bakit itong maliit na bagay na ito hindi nia magawa? Ang pigilan ang kanyang bibig? Malaking ginhawa para sa ekonimiya natin pag ginawa nia ito, bakit hindi nia kayang magsakripisyo ng konting pride at humility?

Bilang tatay ng bansa natin, di ba dapat unahin nia ang kapakanan ng kanyang mga anak bago ang mataas na tingin nia sa kanyang sarili?

Brad, tama na. Alam kong nakakapagod siang ipagtanggol, alam kong madami ng tao ang mababa ang tingin sayo. Di mo na kailangang gawin ang mga yan brad, magpahinga ka na sa pagtatanggol sa kanya. Naiintindihan ko lahat ng hinaing mo, madami sa mga yan hinaing ko din, at pareho tayong naniwala at nagkapagasa na maaring si Duterte ang sagot sa mga hinaing na ito. Pero tingnan mo sia ng maigi, madami siang pangako pero yun ngang "aayusin ko ang sarili ko" hindi nia matupad, paano pa yung iba? Wag mong isalalay ang buhay mo at ng mga anak mo sa taong ganyan.

Hindi ako suporter ng dilaw o pula o anumang kulay dito, supporter ako ng ating inang bayan. Alam ko sa loob mo ganun ka din, kaya passionate ka sa pagtatanggol kay Duterte. Ang sinasabi ko lang, magisip ka ng maigi, kalimutan mo muna lahat ng bias, ng ingay, at mga sigaw ng kaliwa't kanan,, pula at dilaw. Tanungin mo ang sarili mo, ito ba ang maganda para sa Pilipinas at sa kapwa ko Pilipino? Pag ginawa mo yan, alam ko tama ang magiging sagot mo. Maraming salamat sa pagbasa.

Following are comments generated by above posting in social media:

c1. Same sentiments here. I used to be a staunch supporter, but he is going WAY overboard and is causing long-term damage to the country. The economy is falling, the peso is losing value, investors pulling out.... All this, for the drug war, that other countries tried to do but failed?

c2. All this for his own ego.

c3. Fake tough guy to be exact. It's fine op, there are a lot of people like you and we applaud you for not being blinded. Good on you. I voted for him too.

c4. His bloated, self-centered, egocentric self. He seriously think that the world will adjust to him.

c5. and he asked for another 6 months. Was hoping he resigned by now.

c6. Ako din. I voted for him. Now I cringe whenever he opens his mouth.

c7. Hard to say the economy is falling for my financial analyst friends say it's normal this time of the year pero the rest ng sinabi mo, i could'nt agree more.

c8. From someone studying economics, yes it's usual but not a drop this big

c9. not an economist/market analyst, but this being the worst peso-dollar exchange rate since 2009? Sayang development in the past years if hard earned investor confidence and trust mawawala dahil sa carelessness at machismo!

c10. I used to be a huge Duterte supporter. As in huge. Nung tumatakbo sya, despite all the noise about DDS, and his unconventional ways - nauto din ako. Parang sya yung manliligaw mo na bad boy na feeling mo magbabago pag sinagot mo. Nagising lang ako dun sa rape joke. That was the last straw for me. After that, I couldn't support him anymore. Buti nalang that happened before the elections - I had ample time to reassess my political choices. But he won - and I accepted that. Sabi ko, I will support this president as much as I can, even if he had said something that I was strongly against before. I had googly eyes watching his inauguration speech (kahit na may issue between him and Leni - which I voted for and has been my choice kahit si Duterte pa yung candidate ko,I voted for MDS eventually), drunk with hope that hey, he might just straighten himself up. But it has been all downhill from there. Ang hirap hirap nyang suportahan. He makes it hard to. I'm not discrediting the good things he has done so far. Pero kulang, friends. Mas lamang yung mukhang magpapahamak satin. At the end of the day, we are all just concerned about where our country is going.. and right now, it doesn't look too good. Masakit aminin, pero he dun' goofed. And his diehard supporters choose to turn a blind eye. Siguro sila, abangan nalang pag humagupit ang consequences, yeah? It's-not-happening-unless-it-happens-to-me mentality. TLDR: Once a Duterte supporter, now just concerned about our country going to shit. I applaud you, OP. Thanks for sharing your sentiments. Ilan nalang kayong kaya tanggapin sa sarili na may maling nangyyayari.

c11. Parang sya yung manliligaw mo na bad boy na feeling mo magbabago pag sinagot mo. yep. this seems like it. ako naman i didn't vote for him but when he won i was ready to support him. baka nga magbago. and he does have good points. oo nga naman nobody is perfect. pero garapalan na ang kawalanghiyaan eh. bastos ang bibig sobra.

c12. Ang hirap hirap nyang suportahan. Magbulag-bulagan ka, like most of his fans do. Sorry, i meant supporters.

c13. I really wanted to support Duterte since he is our president. But I can't, he's against my moral stance and I'm not willing to bend it just to get a taste of a probably better life with the expense of someone else's.

c14. Ok lang naman supportahan si Duterte, just dont be a fanatic.

c15. She moves her body like a cyclone 33 points This guy right here. same sentiments. Instead of being pro-Aquino, or Pro-Duterte, we should all be Pro-Philippines. Let us think what's the best for our beloved country. Magbigay ng karampatang pagpupugay or kungbaga credit sa mga magagandang nagawa (and marami talaga within just a small period if time). Pero let us also see kung ano yung mga "sablay" or pangit na galawan ng gobyerno and kundinahin. Ang stance ko dito is ilan buwan palang yung administrasyon, give chance naman kahit paano and let them do their work and also for us.. let us be the change we want to be.. OO, ako din nashoshock sa Bunganga ni Duterte, specially yung recent na Fuck you sa EU.. Maganda na nakikita natin yung totoong taong presidente naten pero tangina kapag sa ibang "TAO" or bansa naman proper decorum.. Ika nga ni Tado "Don't be yourself" kasi yung totoong ikaw ay bastos, tamad, jerk. etc etc. Dasal Dasal nalang talaga para sa Pilipinas ika nga ni Alma.

c16. 13 days ago Instead of being pro-Aquino, or Pro-Duterte, we should all be Pro-Philippines. I'd like to believe you, I really do. However, the reality is we have very few electable good leaders in civil society, and even fewer political parties that actually stand for any principled politics. If you are going to want to give any significant change in the political front, you will have to choose who and which party to give your support. There can be many ways to be Pro-Philippines - take care of your family and impart Filipino values, start a business and improve the lives of fellow Filipinos by giving them jobs, take care of the environment, etc. But we are talking politics here. Pick a side that you believe truly aligns with your own personal values. And defend it. This is the only way the political discourse in this country can be elevated to principled politics.

c17. 13 days ago Exactly. We should have some empathy for all Filipinos. We know how hard it is to live and work here, let alone try to improve things. Which is why it makes me incredibly annoyed when people de-humanize other Pinoys.

c18. Instead of being pro-Aquino, or Pro-Duterte, we should all be Pro-Philippines. This. A lot of countries think that one of the reasons why we're still down low is because we don't love our own country. I'm guilty of this, actually. Although I hoped that Duterte would show us the way how, that's why I ended up voting for him instead of MDS (btw, RIP Madam). Kaso recently I just can't help not to get disappointed.

c19. Respect for admitting you were wrong instead of blindly justifying your choice. That said- He was very upfront about his political agenda during the campaign period. Now some of his ex supporters are acting like they're all surprised about his aggressive political attitude and his foul mouth. He was trashtalking everyone during his campaign, then suddenly people are like, bakit kailangan niang magsalita ng di maganda? Ganyan ba siya talaga? Give me a break. I'm sorry OP. I don't mean to offend you. But that, to me, is a sign of a voter who did not truly do his homework. If only people paid attention to his behavior before voting, then he wouldn't be our President right now.

c20. Absolutely this. This is my same response to someone in this thread. This did not come out of left field so to speak. He is actually following through on his promises with the same brutal methods he's used in the past. He didn't start cursing everyone out when he woke up after his inauguration.

c21. That, to me, is a sign of a voter who did not truly do his homework. People basically voted a meme. "Patayin ko kayo lahat", "Change is coming". Yan lang alam nila kay Duterte. OK naman sila actually kay Aquino pero nung madami nang "nagrereklamo" at gusto ng pagbabago, yun na din gusto nila. "Oo nga. Oo nga. Pagbabago! Woo!".

c22. Well, to be fair he did deliver on "Change is coming" - it's just that the change we are expecting is somewhat different from reality. I just hope he doesn't deliver on the "Pataying ko kayo lahat" completely (nasimulan na sa mga unintended victims ng drug war... if let's say the economy worsens and people start losing jobs, then he may just start having people die due to increased crime rate and hunger).

c23. He's trashtalking everyone except China and Russia, whom he's head over heels right now.

c24. 12 days ago THANK YOU. That's what I've been saying all along. Nobody researched who could solve the country's issues, they picked a candidate and supported whatever crap came out of their candidate's mouth. "I'm gonna vote for him because federalism." Yet Paez, who once authored a house bill on federalism, was nowhere near the top 12 senators. "I'm gonna vote for him because we should vote Mindanaoans. They deserve to be heard." Did Ambolodto make it to Senate? List down more issues, and those who ran who could actually solve them didn't win. Obviously, they didn't do their research. Also, as a friend of mine said, Arroyo didn't run on promises of corruption, Aquino didn't run on callousness, but

Duterte PROMISED violence, so yes, we could actually blame those who voted for Duterte. He promised most of the things he's doing now, but Dutertheists made excuses and still voted for him. Edit: spelling and syntax.

c25. federalism is not good for country. bcoz pol family still exists. they will be more corrupt. lalo ngayon. congress is implementing a bill to para hindi makasuhan ng graft charges.

c26. Yan nga ang matagal na problema, gusto ng mga pilipino ng shortcut na solusyon.

c27. Regarding his foul mouth and trashtalking: *http://www.gmanetwork.com/news/story/565793/news/duterte-on-being\-president-i-cannot-be-bastos-because-i-m-speaking-for-our-countr\y* On my end, I am having issues with his inconsistency. One press conference he said he will cross the rubicon. Next he will then say we need the USA after all. Also, I don't like that his cabinet members always having to explain what PDU30 says on his press conference. Ang dating kasi parang laging hieroglyphics yung mga sinasabi niya.

c28. Well said. Marami rin naman naga-gawang mabuti si duterte pero yung major weakness niya is sobrang sensitive and petty niya. Tama lang naman na tanongin kung may nalalabag bang human rights sa companya niya against drugs. It's a valid question, pero sa halip na sagutin mumurahin ka nalang niya at sasabihing wag kang pakialam. Masimportante ang pride niya kesa sa buhay natin.

c29. His major weakness for me is lack of diplomacy. The president needs to shut the noise and dont just cuss every foreign reporter that he wants to.

c30. Although what you are saying is true, IMO his major weakness is having "utang na loob" to some of his friends.

c31. Which he claims he doesn't have by the way. He doesn't owe anybody anything, remember the "Emilio Aguinaldo" answer.

c32. I said this to my Du30 supporter friends who are now annoyed or angry at him. What is happening now has been said during the election period. 1) Anti US Sentiment? Check 2) Pro Leftist and probably communist leaning? Check (it goes hand in hand with the Anti US Sentiment IMHO). He was Skyping with JOMA Sison, a person considered as a terrorist in the international watchlist. He blatantly admitted this, and stated na "Mabuhay ang NPA" in one of his rallies. 3) Bloody war on drugs? Check- He corrected a newscaster when asked if he killed 1000 criminals. He said no, I'd like the number to be 100k. 4) Pro China Sentiment? Yes, he did say he wanted bilateral talks and was hazy with his pronouncements. If anyone believed that Jetski thing, they're dumb. 5) Lack of economic know how? Check. He said that he didn't know shit about economics. Now, will it ruin the PHL ECON entirely? I am not yet convinced that he will single-handedly do it and I am still quite optimistic with the economy (I should be, my livelihood as a businessman depends on it) :(6) Small town thinking resulting to small town solutions for big country problems? Check. He did say he wanted to remove fucking Calculus from the curriculum of our educational system. As if naman naninibago tayo sa mga pangyayari e meron naman signs na doon papunta nung campaign palang. I am glad OP that you feel responsible, but there is no need for an apology; it is your right to vote who you want in a democracy. I just hope that next time, we can analyze more and think critically beyond the political rhetoric. As for me, I am not really surprised with what is happening. Also, I hope I do not get the I am pro-Yellow argument with this comment.

c33. This is one of those times when the words "I told you so" would be so appropriate, right?

c34. I informed you thusly.

c35. 13 days ago I hate to say I told you so. I never wanted to tell that to the Du30 voters- I understand their exasperation under Pnoy's admin. I for one, was already willing to vote for him but had a change of heart mainly because of his Leftist sentiment and voted for Grace Poe instead. I just hope that this could serve as a learning experience for voters and that we can somewhat go through the next 6 years without any major upheaval.

c36. 13 days ago I don't like saying it either, but as you've said - It's all there present during his campaign. That's like a big caveat looking at them in the face. Either you heed the warning, or just follow through. Honestly, it was exhausting to caution people during the elections about the potential risks in a Duterte presidency. And with him now in power, I'd say it's pointless to have remorse or regret voting for him as that ship has already sailed. Since they wanted him there, then prepare to sit tight and wait out those 6 years of whatever is to come. Those who did not vote for

Duterte pretty much have accepted the reality of things, it's about time the others did too.

c37. 13 days ago I hope it will only last 6 years though and not evolve into some dictatorship or single party system state.

c38. Yung mga drug matirx nia, puro palpak, kinailangan pa niang mag sorry. Sa kaibigan nyang nalista. HINDI SA PUBLIKO AH, dun sa kaibigan nyang nalista kaya nya pinavalidate uli.

c39. 13 days ago* Hwag mo lang ilagay to sa fb at baka gerahin ka ng mga produtz.

c39. 12 days ago They have no power here. Most of his cult members use free data.

c40. 13 days ago Not just 'gerahin'. They'll bury you down to your grave until you stop responding.

c41. 13 days ago haven't there been cases where duterteristas actually threatened people in real life about their facebook posts?

c42. 13 days ago yup. a lot.

c43. 12 days ago "addict siguro tong gagong dilaw na to" - brainless dutertards

c44. 13 days ago I wish I could share this on FB..Very straightforward at maiintindihan talaga ng simpleng tao. Good job, OP!

c45. 13 days ago wag. dadami throwaway accounts sa reddit. :)

c46. 13 days ago I actually wanted to put this on fb, but I just couldn't because some of the closest people to me are Duterte supporters.

c47. 13 days ago Well this is an opportunity to find out who are your real friends.

c48. 12 days ago I'm on the same boat as you. My family and all of my friends are pro Duterte. My FB feed has been dumpster fire the moment DU30 decided to run for president and it hasn't abated since.

c49. 12 days ago wag na. i fear for your safety. but at least it is off your chest.

c50. 12 days ago I sent your post to my mom. I've expressed my absolute disappointment when she told me she's for him. I even went as far as telling her that she raised me to be who I am but how come?

c51. 13 days ago Imagine saying this in Facebook and get bombed by comments.

c52. 13 days ago How to loose a friend in one post.

c53. 13 days ago That kind of post is a magnet of hate from dutertenatics.

c54. 11 days ago I post my sentiments on FB I think around July and all my friends and family know I am against d30's ideology. I blocked some of my so called friends who have left the coalition of reason and are just blinded by d30. It does take a load out of my chest that I let out my sentiments and fears about him but also my friends look at me differently but at least I feel free.

c55. 13 days ago You remind me of my piano teacher. He's a very big Digong supporter - to the point that he doesn't give fuck about the innocents getting endangered by the drug-related killings. As long as it gets the job (peace and order) done, he's fine with EJK. But Duterte recent tirades against the US while swooning for China and Russia did it for him. He's realized the "stupidity" of the president's mouth may wreak havoc into our economy. Yes, he recognizes that we must learn to stand up on our own, but he accepts that this needs to be done gradually as many of us depend on the US. More salt on that wound is he's badmouthing his foreign critics when he could just do his job and not mind the noise. Edited: US to Russia

c56. 13 days ago Hey, OP. Nagstastay ako sa Australia ngayon pero involved at informed pa rin ako sa mga balita sa Pinas. Since election pa lang, hindi ako bumilib kay Duterte. I'm happy to see that some supporters are willing to criticize the current situation :)

c57. 13 days ago I have the opposite experience. People I know go through so much mental gymnastics to protect and justify the current president, I think they should all get gold medals at the Olympics by now.

c58. 13 days ago Kabado na nga ako e. Working for a US firm here. I have no idea what to do when shit hits the fan.

c59. 13 days ago Ang laki na ng kaba namin dito sa opisina dahil lagpak ang presyo ng langis kada bariles. Sa totoo lang, mauubos ang contractual workers namin dahil wala kaming project at baka next year, pati mga regular masibak na. Tapos ganito pa ang presidente natin sa US. Wag namang ganito. Mahigit lumagpas dalawang libo kaming workforce dito at mawawalan ng trabaho. :(

c60. 13 days ago I'm part of a team that supports an education project funded by Australian aid. It's suppose to be until 2019 but we we're advised to do everything we could to do transitioning by June next year.

c61. 12 days ago what? oh no.

c62. 13 days ago Best bet natin ay magsialis na bago mangyari lahat yan. Gumawa ka na ng plano para mag migrate, magipon ka na pamasahe. Kung kailangan mong magistay dito sa Pilipinas, do what preppers do. Magtanim ka, magalaga ng hayop tulad ng kambing at mga native na manok (kung wala kang space para dian, buy land using the low interest rates we have today), gumawa ka ng paraan para magkasource of water, stock up on arms and ammo, join or form a prepper group with like minded individuals in your neighborhood. Edit: why the downvotes though? Is prepping still looked down upon here in the Philippines?

c63. 13 days ago Some might interpret your post as you being overly paranoid. Doesnt justify misuse of the downvote button though.

c64. 13 days ago Yup overly paranoid talaga, di ganon kadali ang magtanim or magalaga ng mga farm animals, prepping is fine but a lot of his suggestions were absurd kasi paano kung tapos ka ng law, doctor, nurse, architect, engineer, accounting, IT or police pero ang sinasabi niya magtanim na lang ng kamote or magalaga ng kambing ang option sinasabi niya. To me basta may pinagaralan ka or diskarte di mo kailangan mag panic

c65. 13 days ago Here's your answer OP. Hopefully they are able to realize something from your comment.

c66. 13 days ago hmmm.. actually it's not paranoid for me... I can actually relate (read: the case of Syria and Venezuela). I can believe kasi na folks from those countries were just like me. What he said now gives me another option (worst case scenario baga) by starting to think of a humbler lifestyle... kasi baka in that way, maging masmalayo ako sa attention ng 'powerful' or 'rabid vengeful' folk. Pero pang worst-case scenario lang... tama ka rin, there are other options muna to consider (I love myself some Starbucks eh).

c67. 13 days ago i always found living off the grid appealing. i'm just not sure if it's "safe" to do in the PHL though.

c68. 13 days ago not safe. if you find a remote place to stay, sooner or later the communists are going to come calling.

c69. 13 days ago No problem men. Our great leader is working with China to make sure shit-paying manufacturing jobs are transitioned to the Philippines to replace the ones lost when companies belonging to the great imperialist enemy leave! Sieg Heil!

c70. 13 days ago My famly friend's brother is a call center agent, and I feel worried as the friend and him are the family's only source of income. The friend works as my sister/driver/etc (I don't like the term "maid" since our connection is deeper than that, since she was there since I was 1. She's more of a second mom to me)

c71. 13 days ago I also work at a call center. All my colleagues are 100% Duterte. They even defended him about the rape joke, pope joke, obama joke, UN joke and other 'jokes' he made. I'm hoping that call centers won't close down. :(Ang hirap maghanap ng trabaho :/

c72. 13 days ago Pag nag bawas ng empleyado ang call centers dapat unang tangalin yung mga Duterte supporters. Termination with cause would technically apply...

c73. 13 days ago Not happening. They will cry discrimination based on political affiliation or something. That makes employers who fire employees for merely being a Duterte supporter worse than the employees themselves. load more comments (1 reply) load more comments (11 replies)

c74. 13 days ago Now, we appreciate how 'low key' the Aquino Administration is. Although they had some fuck ups, they did what they promised and that is 'Economic growth'. Years of administration's effort to improve our economy being destroyed by a guy with no long term plans and only prioritizes his ego and friends. I am in no way a fan of Aquino. Every administration has fuck ups but Duterte is on another level. He's a sexist, liar, violent, old cunt.

c75. 13 days ago I've never been a supporter of digong. However, at the last moment, I almost shaded his name on my ballot. I can see why so many support him. He is very effective in lighting up my emotions with his stance on issues. In the end, I went with whom my mentors are voting for. I don't consider myself a smart guy. At a young age, I developed this logic where if there's a smarter guy beside me, it's better to step back and let him drive if I have no idea where I'm going. I voted Roxas because the people I look up to said he's their guy. It also didn't help that most digong supporters, at least in my circle, are the raunchy type.

c76. 13 days ago I voted Roxas very brave of you to admit that. don't be surprised when the duterte shills start targeting you. they hate Duterte's critics but, for some reason, they especially hate duterte critics who voted for Roxas and/or supported PNoy.

c77. 13 days ago That is one of the interesting things here. I wonder, what did Roxas and PNoy ever done to them personally? Their attacks to these two are very low blow and personal that it is almost unfair.

c78. 12 days ago those two were the big targets during Duterte's campaign and continue to be until now. i think it's primarily fueled by Macapagal-Arroyo. she is at least one of the puppet-masters behind Duterte's rise to power. She got really pissed when she lost the elections and was subsequently investigated for her corruption.

c79. 13 days ago I can see why so many support him. He is very effective in lighting up my emotions with his stance on issues. He is a very effective populist leader to say the least.

c80. 13 days ago Bless you OP. I was starting to lose hope since parang wala man lang ba syang supporter dati (or kahit current) na nakikita yung harm ng mga ginagawa nya? Duterte overlord na ba talaga ito? Ang kapalit na ba talaga ng criticism sa kanya ay malaking FU kung ibang bansa ka at character assassination kung Pilipino ka (Hello, de5). Sa totoo lang natatakot ako sa mga tinatakbo ng mga bagay. Wala akong gana man lang mansabi ng "i told you so." Kasi sa huli, sama sama naman natin pagdudusahan to.

c81. 13 days ago Sobrang same sentiment tayo dun sa "I told you so". Ayaw kong masira future ng mga anak natin.

ooOOoo

15.

Why I Publish and/or Reprint Books And it's Free?

By Tatay Jobo Elizes, Self-Publisher

Writings are timeless and they act as mirrors of history. I publish writings as they remain relevant anytime. There are also writers who write a lot but never publish them. There are also old books with no more prints available. The solution is to publish/reprint.

I am offering these services free of charge because of the availability of print-books-on-demand (POD) system nowadays. I can produce the book, but the prints are not free. It's free because I want to encourage writing and reading to all.

Why put your writings in a book? And not just in the internet? I recommend that writings be retained in a hard copy or in book form or printed form for posterity. The book will always be there among your collections or libraries. Not all use the internet. The internet access has its technical problems. Writings in the internet may be erased erroneously. Free storage is hard to access. Paid storage may be returned or lost.

For those looking for a publisher, especially if you have a novel or many essays, I can produce the paperback book under your own authorship at no cost. I can produce art books, family tree books, family albums/pictorials, biographies, joke books, song hits books, travelogues, reunions, color or black & white, etc.

Please buy online as paperback or kindle at **http://tinyurl.com/mj76ccq** (copy and paste to your browser). Permission had been granted by the author/ authors to print their books under my free self-publishing service. They own copyrights to their works. Interested reader may request free reading of any of my books, articles or essays via online reading or ebook. Just email me: job_elizes@yahoo.com My Books Catalog can be seen at www.jobelizes6.wix.com/mysite. The catalogue will grow as years pass by because of additional titles to be published. I continue to publish or reprint books as a means to archive them in hard copy and/or digital form, for posterity and legacy. Thank you.

ooOOoo